BUILDING YOUR CAREER

LAYING THE FOUNDATION TO FULFILL YOUR DREAMS!

SHIVA LAKOTA

TATE PUBLISHING
AND ENTERPRISES, LLC

Published by Tate Publishing & Enterprises, LLC
127 E. Trade Center Terrace | Mustang, Oklahoma 73064 USA
1.888.361.9473 | www.tatepublishing.com

Tate Publishing is committed to excellence in the publishing industry. The company reflects the philosophy established by the founders, based on Psalm 68:11,
"The Lord gave the word and great was the company of those who published it."

Book design copyright © 2016 by Tate Publishing, LLC. All rights reserved.
Cover design by Lirey Blanco
Interior design by Richell Balansag

Published in the United States of America

ISBN: 978-1-68270-211-6
Business & Economics / Careers / General
15.11.13

CONTENTS

INTRODUCTION

What are the most basic things needed to keep one happy? When this question is posed to different people, they will come up with different answers. Some will throw a bucket list at you, and some can blabber on. Compiling a list can become very complicated indeed. Now, think about it: Does the path to happiness have to be complicated? And if so, will you really be happy when life gets complicated? As a matter of fact, when you think hard, you will find that the journey toward happiness is not complicated at all.

In fact, most of us only need a few elements to keep our lives happy:

1. A stable and sustainable source of income, enough to sustain us at all times

2. A satisfactory occupation that inspires us to move forward while giving us our source of livelihood

3. A happy home (note the key word here is *home* and not *house*)

Now, if you carefully look at these three items, you will notice that the first two are absolutely essential to fulfill the third. You cannot have a happy home if your basic needs are not met because your life will become a struggle for survival, and in such a situation, you cannot even think about happiness.

Even if you have a huge bucket list, careful observation will show that all these wishes can be fulfilled if you have these basic elements in your life. After all, you can work on your fancy list only when your basic necessities are met. So the primary task in your life should be to work toward getting all these basic elements, especially the first two.

Now, let us ponder how or what we need to achieve those two items. The answer is straightforward:

1. To have a stable job, you need to be good at some trade or a vocation that has demand in the market. In other words, you need a job that pays well enough to meet your basic necessities. How do you get a job like that? You need to have the qualifications for such a job, and to be qualified, you need the required education and training.

2. To have a job that makes you happy and gives you satisfaction, you need to identify your interests and find work that both caters to those interests and pays well enough to meet your needs. In this case, you need to determine if there are jobs that suit your interests and, if not, what the alternatives are. This is where planning plays a big part in your future development.

Let us now see how to get the third item in the list. You need to have a happy home for personal gratification, or else your journey through life will remain incomplete. What is the use of having a good income and possessing all that you want if at the end of the day you are not happy when you get home? You can be happy without wealth and riches, but you can never be truly happy if your most basic needs are not met.

So how difficult is it to achieve your basic needs? It will vary, from simple to extremely complex, depending on how well you know what you want to do in life and how well you plan ahead to achieve what you want. To be successful in your chosen path, you need to plan your actions and proceed on the path you have laid out. You may have to deviate from your planned path once in a while, but generally, good planning followed by diligent execution will help you achieve your goals. The simpler the plans, the better off you are. Even if you have lofty ambitions, you can keep your plans simple. Often, the simplest plans turn out to be the best.

The journey toward fulfilling your dreams and finding happiness is often a long one, and it is laden with surprises, intrigues, and sometimes unpleasant experiences. You should keep your eyes on the road and not get sidetracked by problems on the way. At the same time, you should learn to enjoy the ride because you are on the path to personal fulfillment and the ultimate diamond ring: happiness.

People have different opinions about happiness and how to find it. However, there usually is agreement on one point: we are truly happy when we realize our deepest dreams and goals. Now, is it really possible to find absolute happiness? It is, but only when you know for sure what will make you really happy and are willing to adapt, be flexible, and to change your plans when needed to get what you want.

To succeed, you need to lay a solid foundation and the groundwork to pursue your dreams. Above all, you need to ensure that your basic needs are met, no matter what. Let us say you are a young man in college and that, in addition to pursuing your education, you also are looking for the perfect girl to date. Now, one day, you find the girl of your dreams and are absolutely delighted when she agrees to go on a date with you. You find yourself in seventh heaven when your relationship blossoms, and in time, she accepts your marriage proposal.

Everything so far is like a fairy tale, but the reality will present itself once you get married and begin your life together. Say during the happy times of your fairy-tale encounter at college, you never forgot your mission in college; you continued with studies and in time graduated with the degree that you set out to achieve. After graduation, chances are that you will get a good job and your life will get happier because, in addition to finding the girl of your dreams, you also have ensured that your basic necessities in life are met. You ensured your professional success by going through the rigors of education and training.

Now, say both you and your girlfriend, while madly in love with each other, get sidetracked, and you both fail to complete your college degrees. You still get married and start life together. You still get a job, but the income is not the same as it might have been if you had completed your college degree. While you still may be happy, all your basic needs may not be met by your income. Then you'll spend a significant part of your time fretting over how you are going to make ends meet. When you have to struggle for survival, you may remain happy, but the daily struggle will become a huge burden.

You can avoid all this if you stick to your initial plans and complete your primary mission while enjoying a blissful relationship with your chosen one. The example is hypothetical, but many such examples exist in real life. Quite a few seemingly happy relationships break up when life becomes a struggle for survival and people need to juggle several things at the same time just to survive.

At the same time, do not ever think that wealth and riches assure a happy life. If that were the case, there would never be any unhappiness in rich families. However, we know that is seldom the case. There has to be a balance in life, and you need to find the right balance to keep you happy.

Throughout this book, we will talk about planning and laying the foundation for a future in which your basic needs are met. Keep in mind that happiness is not a reward that lies at the end of our journey; it is omnipresent, and our lives in general can be happy as we move forward in our journey through life. Barring plain bad luck and unforeseen tragedies (over which one has no control; however, we can find examples of people who have overcome unspeakable tragedies and eventually found happiness), careful planning and execution will ensure that you will be successful in your endeavors as well as happy in pursuit of your goals. Happiness, being ever present, does not mean that you will feel it just like that—it has to be realized, and you have to look for it during your venture. The point is to relish the journey, not just the fruits that lie at the end of it.

This book outlines planning and execution at different stages in your life from when you are a young adult to the time when you are well settled and can continue on your path to greater glory. The chapters in the book tell you how to enjoy the whole experience as you transition from early youth to responsible adulthood. All the suggestions in this book are easy to understand and follow. The purpose of this whole exercise is to show you the means to simplify and enjoy your life. Never for a moment doubt your abilities, and never think about giving up. Remember that you are competing with yourself and not somebody else because the key to your happiness lies with you and not someone else. I hope you find this book very useful and enjoy reading it while gaining a solid footing on your path to prosperity.

Happy reading!

PREPARING FOR A COLLEGE EDUCATION

If you make the decision to go to college for higher education, you have made the right choice, and it will pay off in the long run. There may be times when you have doubts about the value of college education, but when utilized properly, a college degree does pay dividends. It is true that there are some highly successful individuals who never went to college. However, it is highly unlikely that we will be successful by simply mimicking the actions of the successful people who never went to college, for life simply does not work that way. In such a case, going to college is a good option to lay a solid foundation for your career.

On the other hand, there are people with college degrees who are not so successful. That does not mean that it is not worth pursuing a college education. The circumstances of various individuals is different, and when we dig deep, we may find that the lack of success in the case of some people with a college degree may have to do with issues not related to their education. Going to college is a major decision for many because of the expense involved, and many among us have to go into debt to fund our college educations. For those incurring a debt to complete a college degree, any future planning would involve managing and repaying this debt. Going to college and utilizing the education gained toward your benefit can and will differentiate you from your peers and competitors. It is how well you utilize the skills you learned in college that will help to prove that you are different.

When you earn a college education, any plan you make should utilize your college education toward gaining maximum benefit, be it financial or intellectual. In case of a financial benefit, you see the gain immediately in monetary terms. However, intellectual gain too can lead to monetary benefit over time. The added benefit of intellectual gain is that you get a sense of job satisfaction when you are intellectually stimulated. When all is said and done, a college education is a solid investment that will pay dividends over time.

You need to plan ahead and at the same time prepare for contingencies should things not go according to plan. The first stage of planning involves considering what courses you should take in college and how they can be beneficial to you in the future. A more important criterion for this initial planning is whether the coursework you plan to take in college is something that you are interested in. The program that you graduate in may have a direct bearing on your career after college, and the work you do after graduating may be related to what you have learned at college. So you need to ask yourself whether this is the kind of work you envision yourself doing for a long period of time without getting stressed or fatigued and whether it is something that will truly make you happy and contented.

Another crucial component of planning is to explore all means to find the right college and get the funding for your education. Finding the college that best suits your interests is the key, for a good college can help you find employment when you graduate. Stay away from colleges with a poor job-placement record for their graduates.

Once you have decided which colleges to apply to, look for means of funding for your education. Investigate all options available, such as getting a grant or scholarship or any other assistance to subsidize your education. The more you explore the options, the more likely you will get a good deal. You need to pursue and interact with the college admissions committee and negotiate a deal, for in many cases, no one will offer you a helping hand if you don't ask for it. Nothing is better than getting your entire education funded by a scholarship or grant, but whatever little benefit you can derive counts. Taking a student loan should be your last option after you have exhausted all other avenues.

Once you have decided on your course of action and start putting your initial plan into action, you need to think about your second phase of planning. The second stage of planning involves employing what you learn in college toward attaining your future goals and ambition. The training you undergo in college, the relationships you build with different individuals while there, and the process of identifying your true interests all play a significant part in this second phase of planning. The more thorough you are with your plans, the better your future will be.

Planning will vary depending on the coursework you take and the discipline you follow. If you go for an associate's degree with a college term of one or two years, you will have little time to put your plans into action, and you need to act fast. The goal in this case is to find employment immediately after college. The longer you remain unemployed after graduating with an associate's degree, the more desperate you will get, and it becomes harder to find a good job when you are in such a situation.

However, the good news is that short-term associate's degrees typically involve specialized training in some particular trade, and finding immediate employment may not be a daunting affair so long as you diligently pursue the opportunities available to you. Those who go for a four-year bachelor's degree will have more time to work on their plans.

If you go this route, you should utilize this additional time to your maximum advantage toward finding a job that pays well, for it is likely that you will have invested more money in your education than someone who decided to pursue a short-term associate's degree.

Now that we have touched on several elements of planning, we need to explore them in detail. Let us ask ourselves the following questions:

- Should I go for a short-term associate's degree or a four-year bachelor's degree?

- How do I pick the right college?

- What do I need to do to get admission in the college of my choice?

- How do I explore the funding options for my education?

- What should I plan before starting college and after I have gained admission?

- What should I do while I am at college?

Once you have answered these questions, you are well on your way toward a brighter future. If you carefully evaluate these questions and put in effort toward finding the answers best suited to your needs, you will be able to differentiate yourself and move ahead of your competitors. There will be challenges ahead, and there will be times when you have to deal with the unexpected, but good planning with contingency arrangements can help you come out of any situation successfully.

Should I Go for a Short-Term Associate's Degree or a Four-Year Bachelor's Degree?

Each individual's situation is different, and you have to decide which option to go for, depending on your circumstances. Money plays a big part in this decision, and in many cases, parents want to send their kids to college but do not have the financial resources to do so. At the same time, some parents may want to avoid incurring student loan debt that pinches them or their kids too much in the future. In such a case, an associate's degree program may be a good option. At the least, this option gives the kids concerned some form of college education that will help them stand on their own feet and be self-sufficient with a brighter future.

In addition to money, several other factors may play a part in this decision. For example, someone who started working immediately after completing high school may decide to go back to college later on in life. Now, say this person has worked for ten straight years after high school and wants to test the waters by attending a college, hoping it might give him or her a brighter future. In this situation, going for an associate's degree may be a good way to proceed. Here are a few points to consider that can help you decide:

- ➤ If you are a full-time employee who has hit a roadblock as far as promotion is concerned owing to a lack of a college degree, a good option might be to go for an associate's degree program. You can continue to work full-time and attend a community college in the evenings. Two years of hard work will give you the much-needed college education that your employer cannot overlook; in addition, your education will offer you the added benefit of new skills that you can put to professional use.

- ➤ If you have just completed high school and do not have the financial resources to complete a bachelor's degree and at the same time do not want to incur too much debt to pursue higher education, an associate's degree program may be a good option for you. The student-loan debt you incur for an associate's degree is much less than the student-loan debt you would incur for a bachelor's degree. Moreover, the duration of an associate's degree is not more than two years. After completing your associate's degree, you can start working, get your financial situation into better shape, and then think of completing a bachelor's degree by taking additional credits or by choosing any option that looks feasible.

➤ In case you want to start working full-time immediately after completing high school, you can do so and enroll in an associate's degree program. Two years of study while being fully employed will only brighten your chances once you graduate with an associate's degree. The career prospects of an individual with an associate's degree are a lot brighter than those of an individual with no college degree at all.

➤ In case you want to derive the maximum benefit that an education can provide and you also want to get your education out of the way before you start working full-time, enrolling in a bachelor's degree program may be the right option for you. The employment opportunities that you will have with a bachelor's degree under your belt will be far more financially rewarding than the opportunities that someone with no college education or an associate's degree might have.

➤ Even if you have to go into debt but want to invest in a college degree in order to have a shot at a good and prosperous career over the longer term, enrolling in a bachelor's degree program will be a good option for you. The investment you put in to get a bachelor's degree will pay you far-greater dividends in the long term that you might otherwise have to forgo should you opt to not have a college education or should you opt for an associate's degree.

If you are eager to get into the workforce and also want to pursue an education at the same time, you can go for an associate's degree. On the other hand, if you want an education that will serve as a tool to attain prosperity and better prospects in life, you should go for a bachelor's degree. Either way, the chances that will come your way will be far brighter than the chances you might have without a college education. So do make it a point to get some kind of college education, no matter what stage of your life you are in.

How Do I Pick the Right College?

Picking the right college can make a lot of difference to your career prospects. Although many factors are beyond your control, you can still do a lot to pick the right college. Here are a few points that will help you to select the best one:

➤ First and foremost, make sure that the college you pick has a good program for the career you want to pursue. For example, if you want to pursue an engineering career and the college you pick has a good law program but is not highly rated when it comes to other programs, it may not be the right college for you.

➢ Look at the job-placement record of the college, and in particular, look at the placement record of the program you want to enroll in. The main aim of most college graduates is to find decent employment. If the college does not have a good record of helping its graduates find employment when they graduate, then it is not doing a good job. You should try to avoid such colleges, as you might have to struggle a lot to find a job once you graduate. If the college in question has a poor track record in helping its graduates find good employment opportunities but has started making a concerted effort to revamp its career-services division, you can consider enrolling. The willingness to set things right on the part of a college administration is a good sign, and the students enrolled in such a college do stand to benefit.

➢ If you have the credentials, both academic and extracurricular, to fit the profiles of candidates who get into the top-ranked colleges, take a shot at applying to the best colleges. If you have reasonably good credentials, apply to the top-ranked colleges and a few second-tier colleges as a backup.

➤ If you have average academic credentials, apply for admission to the second-tier and third-tier colleges. Good performance in these colleges will more or less put you on a par with the graduates from top-tiered colleges.

➤ If you have poor credentials, both academic and extracurricular, but still want to get a good college education, do not be discouraged. The chances of getting admission in top-notch colleges may be slim in this case, but with a concerted effort, you can get into a college of reasonable repute. Even if you get admission into a low-ranked college, make up for your lack of good credentials with a solid performance in this college. A good performance in a low-ranked college may not immediately put you in the league where you can compete with graduates from top colleges once you graduate, but some employers may be willing to give you a chance when you start looking for employment after graduation. Over time, with diligent effort, you can prove your competence.

➤ Suppose you get an offer of scholarship from any college. Accept the offer if you feel it will benefit you in the long term. Although it may be tempting to take a scholarship offer, it may not always be a wise decision, and you need to consider your long-term ambitions. For example, let's say you aim to work in an investment bank on Wall Street in New York City. You get one offer of admission from an Ivy League school with no financial assistance and another offer of admission with full scholarship from a school that does not have a considerable reputation. You will need to think seriously before making a decision. The chances of your getting hired by an investment bank in New York City are far higher if you graduate from an Ivy League school than if you graduate from an ordinary school, your scholarship notwithstanding. Of course, your financial situation may also play a big part in your decision, but if you find yourself in such a situation and you are a risk taker, do not shy away from taking such a risk.

Do not fret too much about picking the right college. Just keep in mind that if you make productive use of your time in college, you will have a good career. Ultimately, your knowledge and skills will help you prosper, and you can acquire these in any college with a concerted effort. Good colleges do add a lot of weight to your résumé, but ultimately, it is how you market yourself that will decide your future. So if you acquire good skills from a bad college and market yourself aggressively, in time you will still achieve all that you want. In fact, your achievements in such a case will also benefit your college and give it a good name and lift its rankings. Do not simply give up on the idea of going to college because you do not have good credentials. You can always build credentials over time, for it is never too late.

What Do I Need to Do to Get Admission in the College of My Choice?

Just as it is important to find the right college, it is equally important to work on your candidacy toward getting admission into the college of your choice. Gaining admission into a college involves working on a combination of factors and getting things right. After all, it is not just you who can be picky about colleges, the colleges too are picky about who they want in their student body. So you need to make sure that you fit the bill. In addition to keeping your academic profile straight, you need to work on the following criteria:

➤ Besides academics, find out what criteria in particular the college of your choice lays emphasis on when it comes to admitting a candidate into the college. For example, some schools lay emphasis on extracurricular activities and the overall personality of the student looking for admission. Make sure that you meet the criteria, and if you notice any shortcomings in your candidature, work on overcoming your problems.

➤ When you start working on your application, highlight all your strengths and characteristics that you think the admissions committee needs to consider. Project yourself in such a way that the powers that be cannot ignore your strengths before making a decision. There are several ways in which you can display your skills and strong points when you apply to colleges. A few points worth considering are the following:

   o Answer all questions in the application form thoroughly, and in particular, spell out your strengths clearly; do not leave any scope for ambiguity.

   o The college-admission essays will give you a great opportunity to display the strengths and characteristics in you that make you worthy of being admitted. Well-written essays can help you overcome a lot of other shortcomings in your candidacy. Put your heart into writing the essays, and do a very good job. You can take suggestions from others, but the core content of your essay has to come from you. Spell your heart out in your essays.

   o In the answers to the questions on the application form, make sure to mention what you can bring to the classroom in form of your experience, skills, and diversity. Every individual is different, so you need to mention what makes you unique as compared to other candidates and how your unique characteristics will benefit your class.

➢ Work very hard, and do well on any standardized test that you may need to take for gaining admission into the college of your choice. For example, good scores on tests like SAT and GRE can help offset a not-so-colorful academic profile.

➢ Reach out to the admissions committee in every possible way open to you, and display how passionate you are about gaining admission into the college of your choice. College admissions are mostly based on objective criteria, but there are candidates who found out to their surprise that passion can sometimes negate objectivity and work in one's favor.

➢ Do not approach the application process with doubt in your mind, and never let any kind of negative thinking creep into your psyche. If you do so, your thoughts will result in a self-fulfilling prophecy. After all, we all get what we wish for, both good and bad. So go with confidence, and get what you want.

If you feel you are worthy of being considered for admission into the college of your choice, do everything you need to do make the college consider your case. Do not simply go through the motions, but put in a concerted effort and be positive in your outlook. Do not entertain any negative thoughts, and when you are in such a frame of mind, the right path will automatically surface in front of you.

How Do I Explore the Funding Options for My Education?

Exploring the financing options early on while you are applying for colleges will go a long way toward reducing the money you need to invest in your education. It is true that candidates with very good academic and overall credentials are awarded automatic scholarships and financial aid, but the way you approach the admissions process will also have a bearing on the approval or denial of financial assistance. Following up with the admissions committee can often help you get assistance. Here are a few points you need to consider in order to explore all funding options:

> ➤ First and foremost, look at applying to colleges that have an endowment to assist its students financially. Financial aid is limited for most colleges, but some colleges do a better job at this than others. You need to see the track record of the colleges for this, and it will involve some research on your part. However,

spending time on researching this aspect may save you a lot of money.

➢ The awarding of scholarships and financial aid is not always fair, and when you dig deeper, you will no doubt notice that. Here, too, you need to look at the track record of the college. Talk to some students at the colleges where you want to enroll, and find out the information firsthand. You stand to benefit a lot by carrying out this exercise.

➢ Once you have applied to the colleges, follow up and interact with the admissions committee. This exercise can get you some kind of financial assistance that you might not otherwise get. The saying "The crying baby gets the milk" applies here, as you may not receive any help unless you specifically ask for it.

➢ If you have tried your best but could not get any kind of financial assistance from any college, another option is to apply for a student loan. Thoroughly research the various student-loan options available to you, and pick one that will prove to be the least burdensome over the longer term.

➢ Look for student loans that offer you the most flexible repayment options as opposed to ones that can make life difficult for you afterward. Make sure you read all the terms and conditions of the loan you are about to take, and pick the one with the terms and conditions you will be able to abide by without a problem. Every student's situation is different. When you pick a loan, consult with your family members and other well-wishers who can guide you in making the correct choice.

Although money plays a crucial part in the decision on whether to go to college or not, and taking on a student loan is an intimidating prospect for some people, weigh all factors and make the decision that will be of most benefit over the long term. Remember, you get a college degree for life, so it will benefit you throughout your life. Do not let the thought of the considerable monetary investment in attaining a college degree deter you from enrolling in college. The investment you put in today will pay rich dividends in the future, and you can rest assured about that.

What Should I Plan before Starting College and After I Have Gained Admission?

Once you have gained admission into a college, the difficult part is over, and you need to plan the best course of action to derive the maximum benefit from your college education. Simply attending college and going through the motions may give you the degree, but you will face many challenges once you graduate. It is not enough to get a college education; it is important that you be able to apply your education to real life and build a great career for yourself, not to mention a bright, prosperous future. Here are a few points that you need to consider:

> Plan the courses you want to take. Some courses are mandatory based on your discipline or major. However, you will have a lot of say in picking your elective courses. Although you may not have to decide about your elective courses in the first or second year of college, having a plan early on would not hurt.

> Think about your interests today before you start college. When you make plans, leave some leeway in case your interests evolve and change over time. See how best you can utilize your coursework to fulfill your career ambitions.

> Take a look at the extracurricular activities the college offers, and decide which ones you want to participate in. In addition to your academics in college, your extracurricular activities can go a long way toward shaping your career.

> Make a timetable for yourself, and be prepared to stick with it. Set some time aside for self-study, group study, and extracurricular activities besides your mandatory classwork, and you will find the going very easy. Create a plan that allows you the

maximum flexibility and lets you enjoy the whole college experience.

> Do some research on the college faculty, and see how best you can utilize them to attain your goals. For example, if a faculty member has a good reputation in your field, look at the opportunity of doing some kind of project under his or her guidance.

> Make it a point to see how what you learn in class is applicable to real life. The ability to apply your classwork to real-life situations will ultimately decide your success in life after college. Gear your mind toward finding the real-life applicability of what you learn in class, and you will find your coursework all the more interesting.

No matter what plans you make, be flexible and open to new ideas. Your interests may evolve over time, and being adaptable will leave you with plenty of options to choose from. Do not be resistant to change, and if changing your habits in some way benefits you in the long term, be ready to do so without any trepidation.

If you go to college immediately after completing high school, treat your college life as an adventurous journey leading to adulthood, and you will find the experience enriching. On the other hand, if you are going back to school later in life, treat your college life as a long-term project, the successful completion of which can lead you to great places, and you will still find the experience enriching. Plan ahead and be adaptable, and you will be well on your way to tasting success.

What Should I Do While I Am at College?

This topic will be discussed in detail in chapters 4 and 5, but I would like to stress a few points here:

> ➤ Going to college is not just about getting an education and obtaining a degree. Your education in college is not limited to your coursework; it also involves building and developing your personality. The more you participate in extracurricular activities and interact with a variety of individuals, the better your future will be.

> ➤ Build relationships with your classmates, teaching faculty, and others. The more you interact with people, the better your people skills. These skills are an invaluable tool that can take you places. Most successful individuals have very good people skills, and college is a good place to build, test, and develop them.

> ➤ Make it a point to attend career fairs and talk to the representatives of various companies present there. These interactions are a good way to network and will serve you as a valuable investment for the future.

You can sometimes count on your networks to help you in your future job search. Besides helping with finding a full-time job, you can sometimes count on your networks for a good internship during the long breaks you have while at college.

➢ Try to work part-time whenever and wherever possible while you are at college. These part-time jobs or internships will give you invaluable experience that you can apply to full-time jobs when you eventually start working full-time after graduating from college. If nothing else, these part-time jobs will give you your own income, and you will start appreciating the self-respect that you can derive as a result.

In addition to the points mentioned above, be prepared to do anything that you think will benefit you in the long term. Talk to student counselors, career counselors, and anyone you think can help you. Seek help whenever needed, and be open to suggestions. Just as it is never too late, it is never too early to plan for your future and to put those plans into action.

No matter what stage of life you are in, you can always think about going to college if you do not have a college education yet, for it is never too late. An eighty-year-old graduating with a college degree will feel just as happy as a twenty-year-old with the same accomplishment. If you have completed your college education, always plan ahead. No matter how old we are, we are never fully grown up. There is always something somewhere that seems like an attractive proposition worth pursuing. So plan ahead, and you will find happiness at every step in your journey through life.

PURSUING A SHORT-TERM
COLLEGE PROGRAM

A short-term college program is a good option for someone who wants to get a college education but does not want to spend too much time or money on something for which the benefits are not immediately known. Some people are skeptical about the benefits of a college education and are not convinced that lack of a college education will restrict progress in their careers. When these people eventually decide to take a shot at college, many of them take baby steps by opting for a short-term program to test the waters. Typically, the following types of people will find a short-term program beneficial:

1. People who have hit a career-advancement road-block owing to lack of a college degree. It is common to see talented people stuck in limbo because

they do not have the qualifications deemed necessary to get promoted above a certain level.

2. People who have kept their plans for higher education in abeyance and decided not to pursue higher education immediately after high school, depending on individual circumstances.

3. People who want to get some form of college education but are unsure of its benefits until they experience them firsthand and hence do not want to expend many resources (time, money, energy, etc.) for it.

4. People who want to get an education but are not in a position to spend much time or incur a great expense as may be incurred by completing a traditional college program.

5. People who want to experience the benefits of higher education in a short period of time before venturing into a long-term degree program.

Of course, other people have reasons other than those mentioned above to opt for a short- term college program. But one thing is certain: a college degree will not do you any harm if you are careful. It may give you debt from student loans, but careful and tactical utilization of the skills you gain in the process will stand you in good stead and leave you with a lot more after paying off your student-loan debt.

For example, there are some high-paying jobs that require you to possess a college degree. Say you are looking for one such job and take a student loan to complete your degree and eventually get the job. Would you not be better off in your life ahead in spite of taking a student loan? Before you step into a short-term program and as you pursue your education, you need to plan ahead. Here are a few pertinent questions that you may need answers to as you go about this exercise:

- What kind of approach should I take as I venture into a college program?

- What do I need to do to grasp the concepts of what I learn?

- How should I utilize my time outside of study?

- How do I utilize my skills toward attaining my goals?

- What kind of working and professional relationships should I build, and how do I take advantage of these relationships for a better future?

- How do I plan my job search while I am at college and when I approach graduation?

- What options should I explore after college?

Once you devote time to finding answers to these questions that are best applicable to you, you will find the direction to your goals. Just have faith and confidence in your abilities, and you will find the sailing smooth and your journey will give you the desirable end results. Let us see how best we can get you on track by looking for answers to these questions.

What Kind of Approach Should I Take as I Venture into a College Program?

Remember, when you decide to pursue a higher education, it is because you expect it to open new doors to future prosperity. You always must be open to ideas in this venture. Your intent should be to make sure that the whole exercise you have undertaken bears the fruit you desire and doesn't simply go to waste. It will go to waste only if you fail to make everything count. Keep the following points in mind as you progress in your endeavor in college.

> Be enthusiastic in what you do, and treat the whole exercise as a challenge that will leave you better off than you were before you started college. Never think that this whole exercise may not be useful in the long run. The moment you start thinking that way, you will initiate a self-fulfilling prophecy that will eventually lead to a result that was never your intention but something you dreaded all along.

> Show eagerness to learn new things, whether in your classroom or from the books that form part

of your curriculum. Never think that you may not learn anything new.

➤ Your mind may be used to certain kinds of ideas, and you may be used to doing things in certain kinds of ways, and there is nothing wrong with that. However, be prepared to learn new ideas and new ways to do things that will aid your own ideas. When you are enthusiastic about learning new things, you can help yourself do things more efficiently. Resistance to new ideas only makes it more difficult to learn them. I have seen people who are used to doing things a certain way and often complain about how much effort they have to put into getting their tasks done. However, when they come across new and efficient ways to complete the same tasks, they are resistant to change and find some excuse not to try out new ideas. Thus, their drudgery continues unabated. Do not fall into this kind of trap; be open to ideas, and learn to adapt.

➤ In addition to the courses you take, learn new things via a hands-on approach by doing projects wherever possible. Learning by doing ensures that things stay in your mind for a long time, while simply reading about them may lead you to forget them as soon as your exams are over.

➢ In addition to coursework and project work, look for means to enhance your career prospects as a result of your newfound skills. Talk to career counselors or anyone whom you think might be able to help you find brighter prospects after you graduate. The more you network with different individuals, the better off you will be. Otherwise, you may live in your own shell and come out of college only with a diploma.

➢ Even if you pursue a college education while working in a full-time job, never let go of any opportunity that promises a brighter future than what your current job promises after you graduate. Some people who pursue higher education while working full-time overlook other opportunities, thinking that they will consider them once they complete their education because they are employed now and may be promoted once they graduate. However, things can change as time goes by, and it may prove difficult to redeem a lost opportunity later on.

➢ Be prepared to advertise yourself and stress your newfound skills when you look for new avenues of employment after graduation. If you do not stress your skills, potential employers may not know about them. You can mention them in your résumé, cover letter, or job application.

Remember, the more you learn, the better off you are, provided you are open to ideas and are prepared to utilize the skills you learn. No one is going to take notice of you simply because you have a college degree, but they will notice when you utilize the skills you learn in college to the optimal benefit in your job. Go in with an open mind, develop an adaptive nature, and learn all that college presents to you. As you do, you will ascend to a new pedestal.

What Do I Need to Do to Grasp the Concepts of What I Learn?

You may not realize it and it may not be obvious, but there are many ways to grasp the concepts of what you learn. You don't have to memorize everything you read, but you need to ensure that you understand the concepts behind what you read and that the fundamentals of what you learn stay with you. If nothing else, make sure that the subject matter of the courses in your major stays in your mind.

The point is, when you understand and retain the subject matter, you may not remember everything. The next time you come across a similar subject matter or its real-life application, the concept that you learned will come back, and you will understand everything more clearly.

Let's look at a simple example and its relation to real life. Archimedes's principle and the laws of flotation state, "Any object wholly or partially immersed in a fluid is buoyed up by a force equal to the weight of the fluid displaced by the object." When read in isolation, this may not make any sense at first. Stated simply, all it means is that if the weight of an object placed in a fluid (such as water) is less than the weight of the fluid it displaces, it will stay afloat. If the weight of the object is more than the fluid it displaces, it will sink.

Even with this explanation, the concept may still not make sense to some people. Suppose you are one of them. What should you do to make sure not only that you understand it but also that it stays in your mind?

Think of a real-life example where Archimedes's principle is in play: a cruise ship. It is huge and has hundreds of people on board with all the amenities someone on a holiday might need. Yet it sails on water. The reason this is possible is that the weight of the cruise ship and all aboard it is less than that of the seawater it displaces.

Of course, there is a lot more to Archimedes's principle, but the point is that when you read any subject matter, you should try to relate the concept to real-life examples. Then it will be easy for you to understand.

Here are few things to try out to make sure what you study stays in your mind:

> First and foremost, understand what you read. Do not simply memorize it for your exams. Memorizing subject matter without understanding it may help

you get good grades, but your lack of understanding of the subject matter may come back to haunt you when you have to apply the concept in real life.

➤ If you find the subject matter difficult to understand, read it again and look for real-life applications of the concept involved. It will start to make more sense.

➤ If despite of all your efforts you still have difficulty grasping the subject matter, seek help from someone who is thoroughly acquainted with the topic. Request that he or she explain it to you with relevant examples. Do not let your ego get in the way of seeking help. Also, keep in mind the old saying that "no question is a silly question, only the one that has not been asked."

➤ Some concepts are introduced into your coursework to sharpen your thinking more than anything else. Understand what the course content is used for in real life, and things will become clearer. For example, the math formula $(a + b)^2 = a^2 + 2ab + b^2$ may not find much use in real-life applications. However, when you exercise your mind by going through the rigors of learning and understanding these kinds of formulas, you sharpen your mental faculties. Later on in life, if you come across complex equations as part of your job function, you will have no problem in dealing with the situation. So in addition to understanding the course content, try to understand the intent of the course. You will start seeing things from a different and brighter perspective.

➢ If you come across any complex topic, do not try to absorb too much of it quickly. Spread your study time across several days, and read the subject matter gradually. The time you spend relaxing between these study periods will ease the burden on your mind, and you will grasp a lot more than if you try to absorb it all at once.

Experiment with new ways to do things to understand what you read, and ensure that it stays in your mind. There are no hard-and-fast rules, and each individual can find a different strategy to understand and absorb the course content. Just do so with dedication, and think about all the good things that might result when you eventually graduate. Believe me, knowledge is power, and someone with knowledge will always be a step ahead of the competition. It is the knowledge capital that the United States possesses more than anything else that has made it a world superpower.

How Should I Utilize My Time Outside of Study?

Proper utilization of time outside of study can go a long way toward shaping your future. Relaxing and taking some time off is essential, but do not spend all your spare time doing nothing. Extracurricular activities that you participate in have a bearing on your future. Time well spent on building professional relationships and networking, as well as productive avocations, can influence your future substantially.

Building working relationships and networking are an art, and the better you get at it, the more your future will be rewarded. Talking to different people and exchanging ideas will help mold you into a versatile individual who has all the essential qualities. Interacting with others will build your people skills, which are vital for you to move ahead in your career. Here are a few things to consider doing outside of your study curriculum:

➢ Besides paying attention to your hobbies and interests, try to make it a habit to engage in meaningful conversations with people who matter. Talk to your teachers and ask for their suggestions, talk to your classmates and exchange ideas with them, and seek the advice of counselors who can give you valuable ideas that can help you move forward. Just make sure that you do not indulge in idle gossip with anyone.

➢ Read some books related to your coursework and outside of your coursework. Regardless of what you read, your mind receives intellectual stimulation that sharpens your thinking.

➢ Keep abreast of the current events that may or may not have a bearing on your life. Remaining aloof and ignoring what is happening both on and off the campus can make you a pariah. You need to be social to move ahead.

➢ Take part in activities that can help you overcome nervousness when facing a crowd. For example, participating in debates can help you overcome stage fright.

➢ Above all, use your spare time to work on your weaknesses. Talk to others who do not have the same weaknesses as you, and seek their advice to overcome your problems. That which is a weakness today should not remain a weakness tomorrow.

Going to college is not about all studies. When you balance your coursework with extracurricular activities and fun, you will become a complete person.

How Do I Utilize My Skills toward Attaining My Goals?

Realizing your ambitions and attaining your goals will depend, to a large extent, on your ability to put your skills into practice. You acquire plenty of skills in college; some are obvious and others are not, but all are embedded in your mind. It is one thing to gain skills; it is entirely different to apply them for practical use and in the process derive maximum benefit for yourself and others. Here are a few ways to utilize your skills and derive maximum benefit:

> Whenever you learn any new concept, also learn how it is applicable in real life. Once you see a concept being applied in a real-life situation or apply the concept to a real-life situation yourself, the idea stays in your mind. Whenever the need arises, this skill will be available to you.

> Once you learn new skills and know how they are applicable in real life, grab any opportunity to display your skills. When you do, others will take notice, and it will serve as a good advertisement for your candidacy for any job or activity that interests you. Word gets around, and some employer will notice you and give you the opportunity to build your future.

> Work on projects that allow you to put your skills into practice. Showcasing good projects on your résumé will make you attractive to any employer, and this, in turn, will help you land the right job when you eventually hit the job market.

> If you come across a situation in which you feel that things are not being done the right way and that applying your skills can help, volunteer at once. Opportunities like these are few and far

between, but if utilized the right way, they can boost your career. Showcasing such activities in the extracurricular-activities section of your résumé will boost your image and help you get the job of your choice in the future.

➢ However, only volunteer when you have the time to spare so it is not done while neglecting your studies.

The only way you can best utilize your skills is to put them into practice or know the context in real life in which they can be applied. Venture out on campus, and look for opportunities to use your skills. Once you make a habit of it, you will have no difficulty realizing your ambitions as time progresses.

What Kind of Working and Professional Relationships Should I Build, and How Do I Take Advantage of These Relationships for a Better Future?

To move ahead in life, you will always need to build professional relationships, which can come in handy in your times of need. Do not underestimate the benefits of networking. The time in college is a good time to start developing associations with different individuals and make these associations count. The more you interact with people, the more you build the people skills that will eventually make you very successful in your chosen profession:

➤ Start by talking to your teachers and seeking their guidance to help you make informed choices about the coursework or career path you choose. Always book an appointment to meet with them so you know you aren't imposing yourself on them.

➤ Talk to seniors and seek their advice, asking them to share with you the challenges they have faced. This will help you avoid any potential pitfalls as you progress through your college life.

➤ Take part in any networking events organized by your college. At such events, you get to meet working professionals and alumni who can help you choose the right path.

➤ When you meet alumni or other professionals at various events, ask for their business cards. If they don't carry them, ask for their e-mail addresses. Keep in touch with them once in a while, and seek their advice whenever necessary. This helps to keep the connection alive. Do not simply forget about an individual after a meeting; you never know who might be useful in future.

➤ Remember that people do not like to be disturbed when they are busy, so keep your interactions to a minimum and send out greetings on occasion. This way, they feel respected and will hold you in high esteem.

Always remember that building good relationships can go a long way toward developing a successful career. Never underestimate anyone, and do not stop communicating with others simply because you have gotten busy over time. No matter how busy you are, spare some time and effort to keep relationships with other individuals alive by communicating with them occasionally. You never know who is going to be useful to you tomorrow.

How Do I Plan My Job Search while I Am at College and When I Approach Graduation?

A job search does not necessarily mean looking for a full-time job; it also means seeking part-time jobs or internships while at college. Working in a part-time job while going to college gives you an income to pay some of your bills, and it also may give you the chance to apply some of the skills you pick up in school to real-life situations. Internships are another step in that direction. Holding any job while at school may give you some income, but it may not always make you happy, and happiness is something not worth forgoing. Here are a few ways you can plan your job search:

> ➢ First, go to the college's counseling center that helps students find jobs on campus. Many campus jobs allow you to put your lessons in class to the test. You have to start early and be proactive to

land a part-time job that may offer you practical experience in your coursework.

> If you do not find any job to your liking on campus, look around town; there often are small companies that rely on student workers. Even if these jobs do not give you the opportunity to put some of your coursework theories to practice, they do provide a chance to develop your people skills, which can prove invaluable in the future.

> Talk to your classmates and others in school to see if they can guide you toward a part-time job. Referrals from friends can help you find a job that interests you. In addition, making some money by working part-time will boost your self-esteem.

> When you are about to graduate, it is time to look for a full-time job (unless you have decided to continue your education). In many ways, looking for a full-time job is quite different from looking for a part-time job. First, decide what kind of job you want to do and what kind of companies you want to apply to.

> Once you have short-listed a set of job profiles and companies that you want to apply to, work on your résumé. Do your utmost to create an effective résumé; get help from others when necessary in this regard.

> ➢ When you are ready, apply via the career websites of the companies that you are interested in. It may take a long time to complete each application, but the effort you put in will bear fruit eventually, and you will be happy that you did so.

> ➢ Plan to attend career fairs, and be ready to market yourself aggressively. Prepare a summary of what you want to say about yourself to company representatives, and show them that your skills and interests are a good fit for their requirements.

Planning a job search is about creating a package that is attractive to a potential employer, and in this case, the package is you. When you market yourself, you have to display everything that makes you an attractive candidate. These elements include your résumé, your speech, the confidence you display, your mannerisms, and your skills. Think about all these factors, and plan accordingly. Packaging yourself may be tedious, but the eventual rewards will be well worth your efforts.

What Options Should I Explore After College?

Getting a job after college is not an end goal in itself; it is a means toward achieving long-term ambitions. Life is full of options, and you need to continue to explore these options to attain your goals and, in the process, happiness. When you graduate from college, think of the following options:

- ➤ If you want to pursue advanced studies, explore schools that will give you the best opportunity for the field you want to specialize in.

- ➤ Once you decide to pursue advanced studies, think about ways to gain admission to the program of your choice. These include scoring well on appropriate tests, working on your application, and getting good recommendation letters.

- ➤ If you feel you are done with studies and want to start working full-time, look at the options available to you and start working on your job applications and résumé. Do whatever it takes to improve your candidacy for the job you want in the company of your choice.

- ➤ If you have already found a job, be happy, but also keep an eye on your future. Look for ways to put the skills you learned in college into practice for the benefit of your company. Good performance in your job will help accelerate your career growth.

Think of your life after college as a real-life adventure, and try to derive maximum fun from it. Relish the whole journey, and you will see your life getting more and more interesting. There are always other opportunities, and if you ever feel that your life is growing stagnant, it may be time to look elsewhere. Even if you are happy, look for different options to remain that way. Not doing so can lead to eventual boredom, and no one wants that.

When you go for a short-term college program, the duration between the time you start your program and the time you graduate is usually very short (not more than one or two years), so you have very little time to put your plans into action. You have to be diligent if you hope to derive the maximum benefits from your college diploma. Any delay on your part will leave you with a degree but not the expected dividends upon graduation. So do not waste any time, and utilize the time at this crucial juncture to derive the maximum benefit and a happy future.

FRESHMAN YEAR IN COLLEGE

If you have just graduated from high school, the first year in college is effectively the beginning of your adult life. At this stage, you begin your training to become a responsible adult. College life involves getting the training and laying the foundation to make your journey through life as smooth as possible. After college, when you start working full-time, you begin sustaining yourself without anybody's help. How well you can sustain yourself in your initial career after college will depend on how well you train yourself in college to face the challenges that lie ahead.

Since the first year in college is when you begin transitioning into adult life, this is a crucial time, and you need to devote yourself to acquiring skills that will help you in the future. You should spare no effort at this crucial juncture of your life, for lack of proper effort may leave you wanting in many aspects later on. You can do a lot at this stage to prove that you are different from your peers and competitors, and this difference can help you move ahead. Despite the challenges, you will have plenty of time to have fun. And you *need* to have fun. Many crucial elements needed in later life can be acquired only by having fun— good, healthy fun, not the kind of fun that can ruin you. We will learn more about the fun part later on in this chapter.

While in college, you can learn important life-changing skills and build your personality and character to propel you toward a better life. All this can be done with careful planning. Now don't let the word *planning* scare you. In fact, planning can be quite simple, and often, the simplest of plans are the most effective. The better you plan, the more simple life becomes, and it makes for smooth sailing in all your activities. You just have to stick to the plan and not deviate too much from it. Every plan needs to have a contingency backup, which we will talk more about later on.

When you start college, you are not sure what lies ahead. There is a lot of mystery associated with life when you don't know what to expect, and sometimes, these mysteries make life so much fun. Remember that just as you don't know what to expect or what lies ahead, neither do most of your classmates. You are not alone, and you will learn things together as a group. You will receive plenty of advice and suggestions from your parents and well-wishers before you start your college journey.

Even if you don't agree with everything they say, hear them out with respect, and don't brush them aside. What may seem to be an insignificant suggestion today may turn out to be life-changing advice tomorrow. Someone who wishes you well is someone worth listening to. Once you get into the habit of listening to suggestions, you will find that it makes it very easy for you to make plans. When you listen to others, you learn about their experiences and the steps you need to take to overcome challenges in life. Thus, your journey in life will be smoother should you end up reliving some of others' experiences, for you will now know what to do to overcome some obstacles.

The focus of your first year in college should be your studies, and you need to devote a considerable amount of time to your coursework and make the most of it. Getting good grades is important, but more important is gaining knowledge, for it will help you in the long run. Don't just study for the examinations and then forget the subject matter once exams are over. Try to grasp what you learn and embed it in your mind as much as you can. Once knowledge is embedded in your mind, it stays with you and will come in handy in the future. Remember, the curriculum and coursework of college have been designed after centuries of experimentation and learning. It is a culmination of the experience and ideas spanning several generations.

So how do you plan your college journey, and what is it that you need to do to get the maximum benefit out of your first year in college? Ask yourself the following questions, and try to find the answers. If you develop good answers to these questions and follow the content of your answers in letter and spirit, you will see that you have indeed derived the maximum mileage out of your freshman year:

- What can I expect from freshman year, and how do I plan for it?

- What coursework should I take, and how do I know if it is the right one for me?

- What extracurricular activities should I pursue?

- If I find my coursework very easy, what should I do?

- If I find my coursework very boring, what should I do?

- If I find my coursework very difficult, what should I do?

- What can I do to have fun?

- How do I make sure that when I have fun, it is not detrimental to me in any way?

- What should I plan for during the recess between my freshman and sophomore years?

Answering these questions will definitely put you ahead of the curve, and you need to start working on answers to the first two questions even before you start your freshman year. The remaining questions can be answered during the year, and the more time you spend trying to answer these questions, the better off you will be. The answers to these questions will help you make your plans and make your first year in college an enjoyable experience—something that will benefit you in the years ahead.

The important point here is to find answers that are suitable for you and help you with your career aspirations. Different people will have different answers to these questions, and the best answers for you are ones that will help you develop and move forward. If you put in the effort and work toward developing your core strengths during your freshman year in college, you will derive the maximum benefit out of your freshman experience and be able to differentiate yourself from your peers and competitors. So let's try to find the answers to these questions and see how it can change our lives.

What Can I Expect from Freshman Year, and How Do I Plan for It?

Most likely, and for many of you, this is the first year of your life when you are on your own and need to learn to make decisions on your own. Many people experience a feeling of excitement, and often anxiety coupled with uncertainty, before starting college.

In spite of all the advice you might get from others, you have to experience it on your own to know what it is to be in college. For many people, college is just an extension of high school, and it takes a while for it to dawn on them that what they do in college can shape their future. Some people do know what they are walking into, and such individuals already have a career path planned in their mind before they venture into college life.

It is good to have a career plan ahead of college, but college life does offer flexibility so you can shape and change your career path based on your experiences. The freshman year gives you the foundation in terms of coursework for the things to follow in your later years at college. You should keep one thing in mind before going to college: you have to be a responsible individual from now on and start taking your responsibilities seriously. In order to take your responsibilities seriously, you have to know what your responsibilities are and what is expected of you.

You should expect to accomplish the following things during your freshman year:

➢ Learn about your real interests and the relevant coursework you need to pursue in order to give shape to your career aspirations. For example, you might discover an interest in math or science and can plan accordingly.

- ➤ Know the kinds of teachers you like based on their teaching style, and pick your future coursework accordingly. For example, if you like to be engaged in the classroom via group discussion, you might choose future coursework that is taught by teachers who put a lot of emphasis on classroom discussion.

- ➤ Know the kind of people you can get along well with, and pick your social circle accordingly. You might have a circle of friends from high school, but now that you are more independent, your preferences might change.

- ➤ Find out what extracurricular activities interest you, and make arrangements that satisfy your interests.

- ➤ Decide on your major. Of course, this decision can also be made in your sophomore year, or possibly even later.

- ➤ Think about whether this college is the right one for you. If not, consider whether you should transfer to a different college. If transferring is not an option, consider what alternatives are available to you.

These are a few things you definitely can expect to find answers for during your first year, and you need to go in with an open mind. Now how do you plan for all this? Well, the answer is not so difficult. All you have to do is make a list of your expectations and proceed to find the answers to your questions.

In order to find the right answers, be prepared to talk to the teaching staff, the student counselors, the career counselors, the senior students, and your fellow classmates. As you engage in conversations with different individuals, you will start finding answers for many of your questions.

In addition, the coursework you take will give you an insight into your real interests, and you can move accordingly. Just enter college with an open mind and a flexible attitude, and you will be able to sail smoothly and enjoy the college experience.

What Coursework Should I Take, and How Do I Know It Is the Right One for Me?

Typically, even before you start college, you are expected to know what your major is and what career you want to pursue. However, things change, and it is not uncommon to find people switching careers based on newfound interests. So do not fret too much over this issue. Normally, when you pick a major, there are a few mandatory courses and a few optional courses. Now sometimes, these optional courses can shape your career. By the time you finish high school, it is more than likely that you will know what you are interested in, but you may not know how your interests might shape your career. The best course of action is to start college by taking the courses you are interested in, and then take the next step forward. Here are a few guidelines that might help you decide on your right course of action:

> Start college by enrolling in courses that seem interesting to you. Once you start classes, explore the career opportunities that you might have after college if you continue with your coursework.

> If your interest in the coursework you picked continues as time progresses, it means that you have made the right choice. Now all you have to do is to find out how these courses can shape your career. You can do this by talking to your teachers, senior students, and various counselors available in your college.

> If at any time you feel that the coursework you picked is not the right one for you and that your preferences have evolved over time, give a thought to your newfound interests, and see what options are available.

> If you find your coursework not to your liking and it is not too late to drop out, do so, and enroll in courses you find more interesting.

> If you find your coursework not to your liking but it is too late to drop out without penalties, continue through the semester, and then make plans to pick

coursework to your liking for the next semester. This may not be too difficult, and you can get the right information by talking to the counselors.

➢ No matter what you try to major in, there may always be some courses that you like less than others. However, these should be the exception and not the norm. If you find all your coursework uninteresting and dull, it means you should think seriously about the alternatives available.

Ultimately, your interests will determine the right coursework for you. You can make a career out of any major that you pursue. For some courses, there may be a lot of demand in the job market, and for some, you may need to work extra hard to find a good job after college. However, you should ultimately do what makes you happy and not follow the herd.

What Extracurricular Activities Should I Pursue?

Extracurricular activities are the key components of character building. More than your coursework, it is the extracurricular activities that will shape your character. When you participate in extracurricular activities, you interact with individuals other than your classmates, and this builds your social skills. Social skills play a crucial role in professional life, and participating in extracurricular activities can help you acquire this very valuable attribute. Here are a few guidelines for picking the extracurricular activities that are suitable for you and ones that can help in your progress:

> Identify your key weaknesses, and begin by participating in extracurricular activities that will help you overcome your weaknesses. For example, if you think that your public speaking skills leave a lot to be desired, you can take part in debates, group discussions, focus groups, and so on, as all these can help improve your interpersonal communication skills.

> Besides working on your weaknesses via extracurricular activities, participate in activities that you think might give a boost to your future career. For example, if you have an interest in going into public service in the future, you can join a debating club to improve your debating skills.

> Besides working on your strengths and weaknesses, some kinds of extracurricular activities are beneficial to everyone. For example, if you want to be physically fit but feel too lazy to go to a gym on your own, you can join clubs where people get together and work out in groups. Having company in such activities might serve as an inspiration to individuals who would not make an attempt on their own.

> ➢ Find out about activities that will help you refine your social skills, and take part in those activities that fit the bill.

> ➢ Attend all networking events organized by your school or otherwise as these give you an opportunity to build contacts and relationships that may come in handy in the future.

No matter what, devote some time to extracurricular activities as these often help you relieve stress. Do not devote all your time to study and in the process lose out on building skills that will help shape your personality and character.

If I Find My Coursework Very Easy, What Should I Do?

If you find your coursework very easy, it can mean either you are very smart and overqualified for the class or you have avoided taking any courses that could challenge your intellectual capabilities. Of course, there are some semesters in college where everything goes by like a breeze. Typically, it is not the case at the beginning of college life. However, if you find your coursework very easy for whatever reason, here are a few things you could try:

> ➢ Get a thorough understanding of the subject matter, and get good grades. Often, people neglect

easy coursework and do not devote enough time to study till exams knock on the door, when it could already be too late. Do not let this happen to you and end up getting low grades in an easy course.

➤ Make sure that the coursework is indeed easy for you. Do not jump to the conclusion that it is easy; you may have overlooked and neglected some challenging chapters. Take a couple of practice quizzes to test your knowledge level, and then decide if the coursework is indeed very easy for you.

➤ Take an additional course if that is a possibility, or simply start reading your coursework for the next semester. If that's not an option, read books on subjects that you find interesting.

➤ Devote your time to extracurricular activities that can help you later on.

➤ Take a part-time job either on or off campus. Doing so will give you some sort of income, and learning to spend money earned by you will teach you fiscal discipline and responsibility.

➤ Keep in mind that even if you find the coursework very easy, you will still learn a lot. You are, in essence, building up your knowledge capital, which will stand you in good stead as you progress in your career. Nothing that you learn, be it easy or hard, will ever go waste.

You can rest assured that even if some courses are very easy, others that follow will be intellectually stimulating and will challenge your brain cells. Take things one step at a time, and do not rush to any conclusion based on the experience of one semester.

If I Find My Coursework Very Boring, What Should I Do?

Now there is a high possibility that you may find some of your coursework extremely boring. Many people go through this experience. It can only mean that the coursework is something that you don't find interesting. At times in college, you will have to take some courses that may not interest you, but you have to complete them all the same in order to graduate. Even if you find some of the courses extremely boring, make sure you put in the right effort and come out with good grades. Here are a few things you can do:

> ➢ Make sure that the courses you find uninteresting are indeed required to major in your chosen discipline. If you find that these specific courses are not an essential part of your major, ask if you can drop them.

> ➢ Find out why you find the coursework so boring. Once you determine the reason, ask your teacher if there are any books on the subject matter that could make the coursework more interesting for you.

- ➢ Take a few sample quizzes intermittently to ensure that your boredom with the coursework does not result in poor grades.

- ➢ Discuss the subject matter with other classmates who may be interested in group study, and see if this interaction increases your interest.

- ➢ If nothing else works, simply endure the coursework like swallowing a bitter pill, and look forward to the next semester.

No matter which discipline you major in, there will be some courses that you would find very uninteresting. In fact, going through such coursework will serve as a good exercise for later in life. There will be situations where you will be entrusted with responsibilities that are not to your liking. However, you may not have any choice but to take up the challenge as part of your duty. College is a good place to begin learning to endure not-so-pleasant experiences. After all, we cannot expect everything to be hunky-dory as we journey through life.

If I Find My Coursework Very Difficult, What Should I Do?

This is a big challenge indeed, and it will test your resolve and character. In fact, quite a few people drop out of college because they find the coursework strenuous and hard to handle. Try your best not to drop out owing to the stress. No matter how hard a course is, there are ways to get through it, and it is up to you to find the way. Here are a few things you can do:

➢ If you find the coursework extremely difficult to understand, talk to your classmates about it, and see if they feel the same way. If most of the class finds the coursework tough and demanding, then you are not alone. In such a case, talk to the instructor about it, and take his or her suggestion as to how you can tackle the difficulty.

➢ Do not read too much at one time. Split your coursework into manageable units, and read a little at a time. Spread your study of the subject matter over several days, as this way your brain will not be tested too much at once. This is one scenario where you can use the principle of "divide and conquer."

➢ Once you have read a difficult subject matter, do not take a practice quiz immediately. Taking a quiz too soon won't give you an accurate idea of how much information you have actually retained. After reading a difficult subject matter, do something else, and come back to it after a gap of a few hours. This way, your brain will get a much-needed break, and you will know for sure how much of what you have studied has gone into your head.

➤ Refresh what you have learned the previous day by going over it in your mind, and then take a practice quiz on what you have learned. If you find your performance on the quiz satisfactory, either move on to the next chapter or read through yesterday's subject matter again and then move on to the next chapter. It gets easier when you read through a difficult concept the second or third time.

➤ Interact with others, going through what you have read and discussing it with them. Talking about a difficult problem with others can often make it easy, as different people have diverse ways of tackling the problem. When you combine the ideas, you may come up with a workable solution.

➤ Often, a course may seem very difficult if you feel a lack of interest. If it is absolutely essential for you to complete the difficult course to major in your chosen discipline, take up the challenge, and see how you can make it interesting. Most of the difficulty lies in your mind, and the way you approach the problem will have a lot to do with making something difficult seem easy.

➤ In spite of everything, if you still find the coursework extremely difficult and unmanageable, talk to a counselor about possible alternatives.

Some courses in your college curriculum may seem extremely difficult. Do not worry too much about it. Make sure that you tackle the rest of the courses efficiently, and then try and get over the hurdle posed by the difficult coursework. A bad performance here and there will not matter in the long run. Even if you end up with low grades in a couple of courses, don't worry, as no one will judge you based on one or two isolated bad performances.

What Can I Do to Have Fun?

Having fun is essential, but all the same, don't ruin yourself in the name of having fun. So long as the fun has no detrimental effects, you are fine. You must have heard the saying "All work and no play makes Jack a dull boy." Focusing only on your studies without any other avocation can have unwanted effects, one of them being that you might become a loner. It is true that many great people in the world were loners, but they are the exceptions, and they did face many issues owing to their loneliness. So be reserved at times if you like, but do try to mix with people and have fun, for at the end of the day, it will make you a better individual.

Here are a few ways to make sure that when you have fun it is more to your benefit and not to your detriment:

> ➢ Indulge in acts that are entertaining, and do not cause any distress to anyone. For example, you can go to movies, hang out with friends, go on a

picnic with a group, or simply participate in sports, charitable activities, and so on.

➤ Do not get into bets that can do harm to you. For example, it is often fashionable among students to get into a drinking contest where the winner is the one who consumes the largest amount of alcohol. It is all right to drink moderate amounts of alcohol once in a while, but consuming it in large quantities to win a bet is not cool. Not only will it leave you with a hangover, but also it can do considerable damage to your wallet. We also hear about alcohol-related driving accidents, and you will do well not to get into a situation where alcohol controls you.

➤ Besides alcohol, taking drugs for fun is another major issue that afflicts many students. No matter what, do not fall into this trap, as the consequences are too drastic even to contemplate.

➤ If you want to bet on something to gain popularity, take up healthy bets such as participating in a footrace or some form of sporting activity that will not leave you with unwanted side effects or injury.

➤ Have fun only after you have completed your quota of studying, classwork, and homework for the day. Fun should only come after you have completed your duties. Do not ever procrastinate on your priorities to have fun.

Focus on your studies first, and never forget the mission you set out to complete when you enrolled in college. Having fun should complement your mission and not be a substitute for it. So long as you realize this, you are fine.

How Do I Make Sure That When I Have Fun It Is Not Detrimental to Me in Any Way?

One cannot emphasize enough that any kind of fun should not get out of hand. We hear about all kinds of unfortunate accidents that happen when people let things get out of hand. While accidents are the extreme consequences, there are a lot of ways besides accidents that one can get harmed while having fun. Learn to draw the line between fun and stupidity.

Here are a few ways you can ensure that the fun you have does not lead to disastrous consequences:

> ➢ Never think that breaking a rule is going to catch attention positively. It could cast a shadow of doubt upon you. Always remember that you can be a greater hero by following the rules. So do not indulge in any activities that are illegal or immoral.

> ➢ Avoid the company of people who have no intention of progressing in life. It may seem that these kinds of people have fun all the time, but you don't get to

see the flip side of their stories when life catches up with them and leaves them bitter.

➢ Do not let anyone provoke you into doing acts that can do harm to you or get you into trouble. If someone calls you a coward because you refuse to partake in an illegal and supposedly fun act, stay away from them. Do not fall into the trap because of your ego. Never let your ego get the better of you.

➢ If you go out to have fun, let someone who cares about you know where you will be at all times till you return. If something goes wrong, someone will know your whereabouts and can summon help if needed.

➢ Do not indulge in any acts that you have to keep a secret. Let your life be an open book so that nothing ever comes back to haunt you.

So long as you follow the rules and have fun, you will be fine. While you are at school, enjoy, have fun, and prosper. Anything you do should lead to your eventual prosperity and not to eventual ruin.

What Should I Plan for During the Recess between My Freshman and Sophomore Years?

Typically, the recess between the freshman and sophomore years lasts for several weeks. This would be a good time to catch up on things that you may not have had time to do during the school year. It is a good idea to utilize this recess in a productive manner. Try not to get lazy and simply remain idle all the time. Do take a small break to refresh yourself, but do not waste the whole time doing nothing.

Here are a few things you can consider doing during this break:

➢ Look for a part-time job or an internship if possible, as this will give you valuable experience and firsthand knowledge of what you can expect after you finish college.

➢ If you want to continue your intellectual pursuits, you can enroll in some summer courses that may be of interest to you. Taking summer courses helps you take some load off your schedule in the sophomore year. You can then utilize the slack in the sophomore year for some productive purposes, depending on the situation.

➢ Travel to exotic locations and try new things. Traveling on your own will help you learn the essence of being self-sufficient, which can be a good exercise in character building.

➢ Enroll in some kind of adventurous activity, such as a summer camp. This can also be a good exercise in character building and can impart life skills that may come in handy later on in life.

➢ You can also use this time to pursue some of your hobbies you may have neglected.

No matter what you do during your summer vacation, do not waste the whole time by not doing anything. If you remain unproductive, you will find life that much more difficult once the sophomore year starts and you get back into the hectic schedule of schoolwork again.

Treat the freshman year in college as an adventure in life, and enjoy the whole experience. When you treat it as a challenge and relish the journey, you will come out of your freshman year a more enriched person. The key to differentiating yourself from others and building your unique identity is to work on and develop your strengths, and the freshman year is a good starting point for this brand-building exercise. The brand in this case is you, and the more time you devote toward building the brand that defines you, the more you will be different.

SOPHOMORE YEAR IN COLLEGE

The second year in college is the time when you start deciding on the best course of action for your future. During the sophomore year, you find out where your real interests lie. So if you are still indecisive about which direction to go career-wise after your first year, you are just fine, and there is no need to worry.

College is the time when you evolve as a person, and it is the time that shapes your future. The first year in college gave you the time to interact with different people, both among your classmates and outside of school. By the time you are in the second year, you will most likely have found friends or acquaintances who share your thoughts and beliefs.

As far as your coursework is concerned, the second year is when the foundation is laid out for the courses that will follow in the third and final years of college. In a way, this is an extension of the first year. In the first year, the coursework you undergo is like an introduction to advanced courses that you may not have come across in your earlier schooling.

In the second year, the introduction continues but with more intensity. You are now exposed in greater detail to the core content of some of the courses that will follow later on. Your coursework will help you determine what it is that you are interested in and what you want to do in the future. Determining your interests is crucial to developing your skills and strengths.

The best way to differentiate yourself from your peers and competitors is to develop your strengths into potent weapons and to work on your weaknesses to bring them to manageable levels so that they do not stand out. The sophomore year in college will give you the opportunity to develop yourself into a competent individual. So this is a good time in your life to make some serious decisions.

A lot of confusion prevails in one's mind during college. This is not unusual. When you look around, you will find that there are plenty of other people in the same boat. One of the reasons for confusion is that you are exposed to many different facets of life in college all at one time, and you have a hard time making sense of what is going on. Except for those who have gone to boarding schools, this is the first time in your life that you are living on your own. Up until now, your community has been the one that your parents built around you.

Now you are on your own to make your own decisions, for more likely than not, you no longer live with your parents. Now the atmosphere around you is different, and you need to build your own circle of friends and acquaintances, for the ones from childhood have moved on to blaze their own paths, just as you are doing for yourself. Added to this, you are exposed to different brand-new coursework as part of your curriculum, and you have to put in extra effort to learn it. Besides this, you have to create your own space and build your own identity—something that will shape your future and take you along your chosen path.

In addition, you now have a new circle of friends who are infusing you with different ideas. All these aspects of your life, when compounded together, can lead to a great deal of confusion from which you have to extricate yourself and define your interests and career path. So as it is for most things in life, you need to carve out a plan and strategy to tackle various issues that are plaguing you at this point.

The second year of your college life is a good time to ask yourself and find the answers to the following questions:

- What have I learned in my first year at college?
- What are my new interests, and how have my interests changed?
- Based on my interests, what course of action should I take?

- How do I know that the path I am deciding to pursue is the right one?

- What is my backup plan should the path I decide to pursue not be the right one?

- What should I do when my second year at college comes to an end?

The answers to these questions may not resolve all your problems, but a careful evaluation of the answers will put you on the right path. Remember, there is no right or wrong answer for any of these questions. The answers are more subjective than objective, but when you spend time in trying to find answers to these questions, a good number of ideas will come to mind, and you can utilize them to help you forge a path for your career.

How well you define your career path and goals holds the key to how well you can differentiate yourself from others and brand your own identity in the future. So spend some time on these questions, and help yourself find the right direction. Let us see how best we can find answers for these questions in order to create a brand that uniquely identifies you.

What Have I Learned in My First Year at College?

You may not even realize it, but you learn a lot in your first year at college. In a way, it is a continuation of high school learning, but at the same time, it is different. In high school you learn to ease your way into college, while at college you learn things to help you with life. So in a way, you learn life-building skills at college, and your entire college education is geared to ease your journey into adulthood and help you stand on your own feet.

Here are a few things that the first year in college teaches you:

> You learn to live independently with minimal supervision from elders. Bear in mind that for some of you, the first year in college may have been the first time you are living on your own and outside the shadow of your parents. Even if you went to a boarding school earlier on in your life and lived away from your parents, in a boarding school you are always under the supervision of wardens or some other staff. At college, however, you are more likely not under the supervision of anyone.

> You gain the ability to make decisions on your own with little or no help from others. When you live on your own outside the shadow of your parents, you will probably need to make most decisions on your own. Earlier, you might have hollered for help when your parents were within hearing distance. Now, rather than call them every time you need some advice, you have likely learned to make decisions on your own.

> Although you may have taken some of the courses before, the content is now geared toward training you for real-life application in addition to teaching you the fundamental concepts of some advanced topics. The coursework in your high school was geared toward teaching you the concepts more than teaching you their applicability to real life.

> The first year in college would have made you a more mature individual. You are now more concerned with standing on your own feet and creating an identity for yourself than you may have been before.

> The meaning of responsibility is clearer after completing your freshman year in college, as up until now most of your actions may have been dictated or supervised by your parents. Being on your own builds in you the discipline and responsibility needed to succeed. You are now more ready to face the world than you were a year earlier.

You may not even realize this, but your personality will have undergone a sea change after completing the freshman year in college. The experience will certainly have made you more assertive, and some of the childhood pranks you may have indulged in earlier in your life will have taken a backseat, giving way to adulthood. From here on, you need to look forward to the future and welcome life with all its complexity and simplicity that make it so wonderful.

What Are My New Interests, and How Have My Interests Changed?

Known or unknown to you, some of your interests will have changed in the course of one year that you spent at college. Being on your own diminishes the interest in some of the things that might have captivated you earlier. For example, kids typically dream about being independent and being able to do things without being supervised by parents or elders. The very thought of being on their own fascinates them to no end.

When these kids eventually go to college, they get to experience firsthand how it feels to be independent. However, over time, the initial euphoria they feel at being left on their own diminishes significantly. They may be happy to be independent, but by the end of the freshman year, they take their independence for granted, and it becomes a routine affair.

Your new interests are shaped by your surroundings, and some of them are a direct result of the company you keep in college. Unbeknownst to you, the following factors influence and shape your interests in your freshman year, and if you take time to examine how some of your interests may have changed in the past year, you can't help noticing the difference:

> ➤ The ambience of the college you attend, the classroom experience of interacting with your

classmates, your teachers, and your coursework will all influence your interests. This new scenario will give rise to new interests that replace some of your existing ones.

➤ Being on your own and being able to make your own decisions with limited supervision will also have a bearing on your interests. Some of the things that may have looked appealing to you earlier in your life may not look so appealing anymore. There may have been things you wanted to do on your own and that may have been out of bounds for you while you were living with your parents. For example, going to late-night parties may not seem as appealing if you have the freedom to do so without anyone supervising you. The newfound liberty to decide on your own for yourself can make some interests that were hitherto unacceptable look less appealing now that they are no longer taboo.

➤ Besides these previously forbidden interests, other more relevant interests will also undergo changes. You may develop a new interest in some courses based on your classroom experience. For example, there are people who fear public speaking. However, a couple of good experiences with a good instructor may generate in these people a new liking for public speaking. This experience can lead them to move on to a career that calls for public speaking skills. This is the typical case of a dormant interest manifesting itself in an individual when the opportunity strikes.

➢ Some of your new interests will be shaped by the student pool in your class. As you are exposed to new activities based on your interactions with your classmates and other students, you will start developing new interests. The interests that you develop now have a bearing on your future, while your childhood interests may have been geared more toward having fun.

➢ Apart from all these, the intensity of the coursework may curb some of your interests, as you may not have much time to devote to your interests outside of school. Some interests that are limited for a period of time owing to work pressure may cease to be interests after a while.

➢ Getting your driver's license while at college or just before college and the ability to drive on your own will also give rise to new interests now that distances may not matter as much as they did in your childhood.

It is normal for interests to change over time, especially when you start your adult life, which typically coincides with the start of your college life. If you do a self-assessment at the end of your freshman year, you will notice the change in your interests. Some interests, which are your core interests, may not change, but some of the fleeting and less significant interests from childhood will definitely take a backseat.

Based on My Interests, What Course of Action Should I Take?

Some of your newfound interests acquired during your first year in college may shape your career. To satisfy your interests while making sure that your interests are taken into account in deciding your future, you need to take adequate steps. You may have found a liking for some courses during the freshman year and want to continue with academic coursework that caters to your interests, both new and old.

Before you do that, however, you need to make sure that the direction that you now want to head is indeed the right one for you, and you should also make sure this direction holds a bright future for you.

Here are a few things you need to consider that might help you decide about your future course of action:

➤ You have now completed one year in college, and by now, you should be able to determine whether this college is the right one for you. If you think for some reason that this college may not be right, look at the option of transferring to a new college. If that is not a possibility, you have to find out how you can make the best use of this college degree for your future, even though the college may not be to your liking. It is not unusual for students to not like the college they are in after spending some time there. However, that is not the end of the road for them. In the absence of any other option, they can graduate from that college and still have a bright future that fulfills their passion and interests.

> If you develop interest in a certain kind of coursework and want to deviate from your previously chosen path of education to pursue your new interest, talk to others about it before making a decision. Professors, counselors, and senior students can help you evaluate what your future might hold for you should you change your career path. You need to take into account the competition in this particular field and whether finding employment in the field upon graduation will be easy. If the field is highly competitive and employment opportunities are scarce, you may want to think again.

> Do a self-evaluation and find out if all your interests were met by the academic curriculum of the freshman year. Also, make sure that you are happy with your chosen academic path. If so, you can continue on your chosen path and prepare yourself for the challenges ahead.

> ➤ If you are genuinely interested in some coursework but find that the opportunities upon completing this coursework are not bright, do not despair. You can either live up to the challenge upon graduation or forge your own path once you graduate. Your passion and interest will show you a way as you proceed. Just do not be discouraged and deviate from the path that you think will bring you real happiness.

Always remember that no matter what your academic interests are, you can make a good career out of them. No course of study will become completely obsolete. The methods of using the tools may change, but the concepts do not. What you learn in academic coursework is the concepts. In the future, it will be in your hands to make use of those concepts, no matter how the tools are molded and how the method of using the tools changes.

For example, a person who knows the computer programming languages Fortran and Pascal will find that nowadays these programming languages are, to a large extent, obsolete. However, he or she can easily transition to a relevant programming language, such as C++, Visual C++, or JAVA based on the fundamental programming concepts they gained via Fortran and Pascal.

How Do I Know That the Path I Am Deciding to Pursue Is the Right One?

There is no simple answer for this question. If you seek the opinions of others on this issue, different people will have different answers. Ultimately, you have to make the decision yourself after giving due consideration to the opinion of others who matter to you. You need to take your passion into account when making this decision, but do not decide purely on emotion and in haste.

Here are a few ways you can determine the answer to this question:

➢ Make sure you are really passionate about the career path you have chosen. Envision yourself doing the work that a person in this career typically does, and determine whether that is something you will enjoy doing for a long time. If that is indeed what you want to do, then you have more or less found the answer to your question.

➢ If, after giving due consideration to all alternative career paths available to you, you think that the path that you have chosen to pursue is the one that will make you the happiest and you do not envision that kind of happiness by doing anything else, then be steadfast in your decision, and do not let anything come in the way of your resolve.

➢ You can take the advice of others, heed their suggestions, and be respectful of their views, but the ultimate decision about your career path should be yours and yours alone. If that is not the case, then you should be prepared for some bitterness in the future, for ultimately, dissatisfaction arises when you continue to do something you don't want to do.

➢ There are some practicalities to be considered when you make a decision about your career path. Find out what avenues of employment this particular career path provides, and learn how the people who have followed this particular career path are doing in their careers. Still, despite all odds, your final decision about your career path should hinge on your happiness. Ultimately, your happiness should override everything else.

➢ Keep in mind that if a certain career path is so obsolete that it does not have any uses whatsoever in the real world, then the courses pertaining to that career path will also become obsolete and will not be taught in colleges anymore. So if you want to pursue a certain career and the required courses are being taught in colleges, then you will find a way that leads to a successful career in that profession.

Do not fret too much over the answer to this question. Do what you find interesting, and continue to devote your time in college to obtaining good academic credentials. Once you get past college, the way forward will present itself to you. Ultimately, you can make a success out of any career that you choose so long as you have the heart for it and apply your mind to fulfilling your heart's desire.

What Is My Backup Plan Should the Path I Decide to Pursue Not Be the Right One?

Even if you follow your heart and pursue the path that you think will make you happy, do have a backup plan. Having a backup plan in no way undermines your confidence in the career path you have chosen. It only serves as an alternative if you encounter too many bumps on the road ahead. Think of a backup plan as your insurance. We all take out insurance plans as a hedge against the unknown. The same logic applies here. No matter how confident you are about the prospects in your chosen career path, you need to have insurance to circumvent any unknown and unanticipated element that may block your path in the future. Your backup plan is your insurance for future uncertainty over which you have no control.

Think of the following factors when you decide on a backup plan for your career path:

➢ Think of how you can deviate from that career path and still meet your end goal without compromising too much. In other words, what are the alternatives available should something go wrong? For example, if you graduate with a degree in mechanical engineering and the demand for mechanical engineers drastically goes down in the future, you can always move toward a career in computers, equipment design, equipment sales planning, or even finance. The math skills that you acquire via a degree in mechanical engineering will help you make the transition without too much of a hiccup. The same is the case with any career path that you choose. When you make the effort to investigate, you will find several alternative scenarios should things go wrong.

➢ Be flexible and open to ideas, and above all, develop an adaptable nature. When you acquire adaptability, you can always find an opportunity in adversity.

➢ Besides adaptability, assimilation is another important factor that can take you places. When you are able to assimilate into any group and surroundings, you will have many opportunities open when the door to your destination closes. For example, in today's global economy, people move to different countries for work. However, some people, when they move to a new location, find it hard to assimilate into the local crowd, which causes them a lot of problems if things go wrong in their chosen path. Now if you can assimilate into the larger populace, you will have plenty to fall back on should things go wrong in your chosen path. Assimilation gives you a sense of belonging, and there will be others who can help you out if things don't work out in your chosen career path. Work on this characteristic right from college onward, and you will notice the difference it makes for you in later life.

➢ Since you cannot plan for uncertainty, be prepared to take educational courses in the future should the situation demand it. For example, when the economy was down after the subprime crisis in 2008 and 2009, some people went back to school either to get an advanced degree or to acquire vocational skills. Now when the economic recovery began from 2010 onward, many of these people found employment based on the vocational skills they gained during the economic slump. Further, some of these people could find a way to get back to their original line of interest when the economy started gaining further steam. Essentially, you need to be flexible and act according to the necessity of the prevailing situation at any given time, and that, in effect, will be your best backup plan.

Develop the qualities of flexibility, adaptability, and assimilation, and you will have the world in your pocket. When you have these qualities, the backup plan will show itself automatically.

What Should I Do When My Second Year at College Comes to an End?

When the sophomore year comes to an end, you are halfway through your degree program, and you will have evolved into a responsible person. Your confidence in your abilities will now be several notches higher than what it was at the end of the freshman year. Rather than get complacent about the situation, you would do well to make use of the recess at the end of the sophomore year productively and in a manner that benefits you down the road.

Here are few things that you can consider:

> ➢ Look for a summer job or an internship to give you firsthand experience of what professional life can be like after you finish college. However, make sure that you get some time off to relax awhile; in other words, do not immerse yourself in work without giving yourself any time to recuperate. You need a breather after the hectic sophomore year, but at the same time, you should use your recess productively. Look for a balance between work and relaxation.

➢ Spend some time finding out information about what your future course of action should be in order to have a bright future. No doubt you will continue with your junior year in college once the summer vacation is over, but having a plan about how you want to approach the junior year will give you a head start. You can plan the coursework and project work that you would like to take up in your third year of college. Summer jobs and project work in college can give a much-needed boost to your résumé, which will, in turn, enhance your chances of landing a great job when you eventually graduate.

➢ If you plan to pursue your master's degree immediately upon completing your bachelor's degree, the break after sophomore year is a good time to start preparing for exams such as the GRE—Graduate Record Examination—that are required to get admissions into master's degree programs.

➢ If your grades for the first two years are not satisfactory, you should be prepared to dedicate more time to your studies and plan to boost your academic scores from your junior year on. That way, your GPA upon graduation will attain some degree of respectability.

➢ If you want to earn a master's degree in a top-rated university for your discipline, you need to think not only about your GPA but also about all the activities, such as project work and extracurricular activities, that will give a boost to your candidature.

> If your performance in college so far has not been satisfactory, do not lose heart. You still have two more years to make up for the seemingly lost cause. Just remember that the core content of your major will be covered in the junior and senior years. Be prepared to slog through it, and you will graduate with flying colors.

Use the recess between two semesters or between any two years in college wisely and productively. Don't leave any stone unturned that might lead you to regret later on. Maintain a positive attitude, enjoy the experience, and work for the best outcome.

A lot of things that confused you when you started college will be clearer by the time you complete your sophomore year. By this time, your ambition will find a firmer footing, and your resolve will also be strengthened by the rigors of two years in college. Overall, your personality will undergo a sea change, and you will more or less have a clear idea as to where you are headed in life.

The most efficient way of utilizing the time in your sophomore year would be to work on qualities and attributes that can differentiate you from your competitors, in addition to everything mentioned in the above paragraphs.

I keep emphasizing this because differentiation is so crucial to creating your unique identity in a crowd. Some people simply go through the motions during the first two years of college and later on realize that they could have achieved a lot more.

You be different and try to make the most of your freshman and sophomore years in college. Just continue to work hard and treat your college life as a journey that will bring you riches in terms of intellectual prosperity, leading to a better quality of life for you in the future.

JUNIOR YEAR IN COLLEGE

The third year, or junior year, of your college life is more or less the time when you will have made up your mind about the career path you want to pursue. This is when you start taking coursework that contains the core content of the discipline that you want to major or specialize in as a part of your bachelor's degree. The first two years in college give you an introduction to the various courses that are available in your chosen discipline, and these courses help you decide on your major.

Mind you, this is the case in countries where the university curriculum is flexible and the students have the opportunity to switch majors without much difficulty in the initial years of college. In some countries, that is not the case, and when students in those countries pick a discipline to major in at the beginning of college, they are pretty much stuck with that and graduate in that discipline or simply drop out of college.

However, even in cases where individuals are not free to make their own decisions owing to parental and peer pressure, they will have opportunities to change their career path should the path they initially decided to pursue is not to their liking. Just approach life with an open mind, and you will find opportunities galore!

The core courses in your third year at college give you an idea of the kind of work you can expect to do when you graduate and take a job in the discipline you are pursuing. This is an exciting time, for it gives you an insight into your future and the kind of activities you may be involved in when you start working. Of course, that may not be the case all the time, for you may find new interests and now forge a different path.

But for the most part, starting in the third year of your college life, you pretty much know where your interests lie and how you want to spend your working life in the future. Since junior year is the time when you start digging deeper into the coursework, you need to make sure that you gain a lot in terms of knowledge. As I mentioned in an earlier chapter, it is not enough to get good grades; it is important to gain a deeper understanding and insight into your coursework. Understanding the concepts will help you get better grades and also come in handy later on in life when you have to deal with real situations. Just remember, knowledge is power and can take you places.

You must have heard the saying "An idea is money," and the foundation to an idea lies in the knowledge one possesses. Many innovations have been carried out by students in college, for that is when they discovered how to harvest the knowledge they gained. It is while gaining this knowledge that they learned how to make money from it and at the same time use it to help society.

Silicon Valley in California is rife with such examples. So when you utilize your time in college productively—especially around the time when you begin the core courses of your major—you will have the opportunity to make a mark for yourself. Of course, not everyone aims to make big money like the successful entrepreneurs in Silicon Valley, but that is not the point here. The key pursuit in life should be the pursuit of happiness, for a happy individual is richer than anyone else.

All the riches in the world cannot buy you happiness, but a feeling of accomplishment upon completing a challenging task can make you happy, and in some cases, this is happiness beyond one's imagination. So this is the time for you to challenge yourself and set new goals for yourself. Accomplishing these goals will get you where you want to go in life.

When you strive and gain knowledge by understanding the concepts of your coursework, ideas will come to your mind, and you can give shape to these ideas by experimentation, which eventually will lead you to a better life. Not all ideas are successful, but then, we have all heard the saying "Failure is the stepping stone to success." Work hard and be persistent in your efforts, and success will find you.

Now what do you need to do in your junior year to make your dreams come true? Let us explore the answer to this riddle by finding the answers to the following questions:

- Is the direction that I am headed in the right one for my future? If not, what should I do?

- What, if anything, can I do differently from what I have already done in the first two years of college in order to propel myself toward a better future?

- How do I know that what I learn in my coursework is retained in my mind?

- How can I motivate myself to do better?

- What should I do at the end of my junior year in college?

When you try to find answers to these questions, ideas will come to your mind, and when you start working on your ideas and put your thoughts into action, you will start getting results. One of the keys to successfully differentiate yourself from your competitors is to give shape to your ideas and not simply let them go waste without ever trying to work on them. Be different and be persistent, and do not let an idea remain an idea. Let us see how best we can give shape to your ideas by answering these questions.

Is the Direction That I Am Headed in the Right One for My Future? If Not, What Should I Do?

Many people face this dilemma midway through college, and if you find yourself in this situation, just know that you are not alone and that it is not uncommon to face this doubt. While in college, you come across different people, all with their own ideas about what it takes to build a prosperous career. When you think about all that you hear, sometimes it can lead to a lot of confusion. Just keep in mind that there are a variety of options available that lead to a prosperous career, and the option you picked is one of them.

To make absolutely sure that the path chosen by you is indeed one that can open the doors for a prosperous career, look at the following aspects:

> ➤ First of all, find out the available opportunities in the job market and otherwise for those who graduate in the discipline that you have chosen to major in. If a high percentage of the students graduating with this degree find a job within three months of graduation, then you need not worry. However, if you find that the demand for this course is going down, then be prepared to face the challenge of finding a job after graduation, or change your major, or consider doing a dual major if you find your initial choice too interesting to give up on.

➢ If you made your choice after a lot of consideration and because you are very passionate about the career path that you want to pursue, then you have listened to your heart. In such a case, your passion and determination will carry you through. However, to be on the safe side, you may consider doing a dual major by taking up another discipline along with your initial choice, or you can take up another discipline as a minor. Remember that if any course is completely obsolete, it is highly unlikely that it will be taught as a part of a regular college curriculum.

➢ If there is not much of a demand for the course you decided to major in and you picked the course simply because you are interested in it, there is no need to worry so long as you are prepared to give yourself a head start. Start by reaching out to various individuals in this profession and to organizations that hire candidates in the field that you major in. You may not get any response most of the time. However, keep on doing it, and someone, somewhere, will take notice.

➢ Be proactive, and do your own research about the opportunities in your field. As you take your own initiative and start looking for a prospective career in your chosen field, you will gather a lot of useful information. In the process, you will gain maturity, which will either result in a job or give an idea and impetus to carve out a career path on your own. For example, there are people who found it difficult to get decent jobs after graduating with a degree in a field they are passionate about. However, some of these people, instead of getting frustrated with their job search, utilized the knowledge gained in the process to start their own business. After an initial period of struggle, they became successful in their ventures and even reached a stage where they could provide decent employment to other people in their ventures. Look around you, and you will find plenty of small businesses born that way.

If you are passionate about something and willing to work for it with devotion and dedication, your journey will automatically be successful. If you choose a career path because you are very passionate about it, then you will find success. Even if doubts arise in your mind about the correctness of your decision, do not waver. Keep working hard with passion, and the path you choose will turn out to be the right one. Just make sure that what you choose as your career is the one that you think will make you happy.

What, if Anything, Can I Do Differently from What I Have Already Done in the First Two Years of College in Order to Propel Myself toward a Better Future?

For those of you who are not satisfied with your performance in the first two years at college, it is very important that you assess your situation and think about what you need to do differently. This is a good time to go through a self-evaluation and make a plan to improve your performance over the next two years. Realizing your mistakes and taking corrective action at this stage can dramatically change your overall performance in college for the better. If you think about it, there are plenty of things you can do differently to improve your grades and academic profile. Here are a few points that are worth considering:

> ➢ Start by evaluating the courses in which your grades were not up to the mark, and find out what led to the poor performance. Specifically, find out if your debacle was a result of the following:
>
> 1. If you think that you did not put in enough effort, you need to resolve that it will not be an issue going forward.
>
> 2. If your poor performance in some courses was owing to your lack of understanding of the

concepts involved, you need to do some studying and make sure that you now have a thorough understanding of the concepts. If you still neglect this issue, your performance can only go from bad to worse, and the consequences will have a lasting impact. Seek help if you need it.

3. If you feel the coursework and the discipline that you picked to major in are not the right fit for you, talk to your counselors about your next course of action.

➢ If your performance was reasonably satisfactory but you want to improve it dramatically to alter your academic profile for the better, be prepared to put in extra effort and plan accordingly. No matter what course you study, make sure you have a thorough understanding of the course content and that the subject matter is more or less inscribed in your mind. More than anything else, understanding the concept will improve your performance dramatically.

➢ If your grades in the first two years are satisfactory and you want to build a profile that can help you get noticed by prospective employers, think of a project work that carries a very high profile. Some projects can make your résumé much more compelling. Talk to your teaching faculty, and take their suggestions in this matter.

➢ In addition to working on good projects in your schoolwork, try to land a good internship opportunity at the end of your junior year. An internship with a great company can do wonders for your academic profile, and your prospects after you graduate will skyrocket as a result.

Just remember, even if you are disappointed with your performance in the freshman and sophomore year in college, all is not lost. You still have an equal amount of time to make amends and catapult yourself into a new orbit. All you need to do is resolve and make a plan to improve your performance. Above all, make sure that you keep your resolution without fail.

How Do I Know That What I Learn in My Coursework Is Retained in My Mind?

It is not necessary that everything you read be etched in your mind. You only need to retain the important concepts that will help you going forward. In your coursework, you will find that some concepts are repeated often. Remembering these concepts saves you time because it is not always feasible to go back and refer to the concept in order to understand the subject matter that you are currently studying.

Of course, at times, you may have to go back and refer to the original concept, but imagine the time you can save if you remember the important concepts and do not have to refer to old subject matter in order to understand current materials. To remember the important concepts in any coursework, they need to find a place in your mind.

Here are a few techniques that might help you remember the essentials of any coursework:

- At periodic intervals, quiz yourself on earlier topics to see how much of the important concepts you have retained in your memory. If you remember the fundamentals and know how to apply the concepts to real-life situations, you are in good shape.

- Suppose you find that your memory is rusty. Read the important concepts at periodic intervals, but read the subject matter as if you were reading it for fun, like a novel. This way, you will not put too much pressure on your mind, and it is more likely that you will remember it the next time.

- Discuss the important course contents with others. When you get into a group discussion, you will find out how much you remember. Moreover, discussing various topics with others will also help you refresh your memory more easily than doing so on your own.

> ➢ Challenge and tease your brain by working through quantitative and qualitative problems involving the coursework that you study. When you work through problems, the concepts involved will become embedded in your mind. A good example is trying to understand the concepts involved in math or physics courses. When you work on and solve a few difficult problems in these courses, you will find that your understanding of the subject matter is a lot better than it would have been otherwise.

> ➢ Suppose any coursework involves the concepts learned earlier. If you do not face any difficulty understanding this coursework while reading it, what you learned earlier is more or less etched in your mind.

As long as you do not memorize all that you read for the *sole* purpose of getting good grades on the exam, you should be able to retain the important concepts in your mind. When you make sure you understand what you read and try to relate what you read to real-life examples, you will be amazed at how much of the course content you can retain. Repetition and familiarity also make it easy. Do not worry too much about how much you remember. Keep a few good books with you for reference even after you are done with the coursework, and you will not have any issues going forward.

How Can I Motivate Myself to Do Better?

The ability to motivate yourself to do better at opportune moments can do wonders for your career and propel you toward prosperity. It is natural for most of us to get complacent when things look relatively stable. However, it is going the extra step even when things look good that will take you places. You have every right to be happy and revel in your success when your goals are met. At the same time, do not get carried away by your success and become lazy. Always keep your long-term goals in mind, and think of ways you can achieve them. One should not give in to greed, but there is no end to the goals one can set for oneself and work toward achieving them. Even retired people set goals for themselves and move forward accordingly.

Just as success can make you complacent and get you to slacken in pursuing your objective, failure too can have a detrimental effect on your motivation. When it comes to motivating yourself, it depends on what state of mind you are in at that time. If you have just tasted success in your endeavor, you will need to take one approach. On the other hand, if you have just encountered failure in your endeavor, you will need to take a different approach.

Let us first talk about motivating yourself when you have met with success in your endeavor:

> ➤ At all junctures, set a benchmark for yourself, and if you are able to exceed your expectations, raise

the benchmark for the next target you have set for yourself. For example, if you achieved A or A+ grades in all your courses so far, think about what you need to do to get a 4.0 GPA.

➢ As soon as you succeed in one endeavor, think about the next one, and if you do not have a target set yet, immediately think about what you want to achieve next, and set a goal for yourself. This will prevent you from getting complacent. If you have achieved a 4.0 GPA in your sophomore year, think about ways to achieve the same in your junior year.

➢ Reflect on the mistakes you made in your current endeavor even though you were successful. Think of ways you can avoid those mistakes in the future and achieve your next goal. For example, even if you achieve a 4.0 GPA in your sophomore year, you might have encountered some areas of weakness.

➢ Imagine the grand prize at the end of your journey. For example, if you achieved a 4.0 GPA in your sophomore year, think about what graduating from college with a 4.0 GPA could mean for your career. It could mean a great job or being granted admission with a full scholarship to the best program for your master's degree. Concentrate on that grand prize, and you will never get complacent.

Let us now talk about motivating oneself after tasting bitter failure. Always bear in mind that "failure is the stepping stone to success," and then think about your next step.

Here are a few things you can do:

> First and foremost, do not go into depression. Failing an exam is not the end of the world. Take a short break, and do not think about anything. If you feel like crying, find a silent corner and shed your grief, as this act will help you take the load off your shoulders. There is nothing wrong with crying in front of others, but you may feel a lot better later on if you can cry alone and away from prying eyes.

> Once you have vented out your emotions, try not to think about what has already happened, however bitter it may be. Simply take a short break and rest as much as possible, or find an avenue to entertain yourself, such as going to the movies or listening to your favorite music.

> Once the mourning period is over, think about your next goal and how you want to achieve it. Think about the mistakes you made before, what caused you to make those mistakes, and how you can avoid making them in the future.

> In addition to setting a goal, set a benchmark for yourself and raise the bar. When you raise the bar, you will have enough leeway should things not go

according to plan. Setting a high bar can motivate you to work harder, while setting a low bar can lead you to slack off. For example, if you want to achieve an A on your next exam, think about what you need to do in order to score 100 percent on the exam rather than 90 percent, the score that will give you the A grade. This way, you have a slack of 10 percent should things not go according to plan. If you plan to score 90 percent, you may end up with 80 or 85 percent, which will land you with a B or a B+ and not an A.

➢ Think about the people who encountered failures and faced a lot of hardship before tasting success. You can derive motivation from the experiences of those individuals.

➢ Always think in your mind, "The worst is over! Whatever comes now has to be good and better." Also keep in mind the saying "Winners never quit, and quitters never win."

Remember that success and failures are two sides of the same coin. You may encounter either of them in your endeavor, but you should never forget your end goal. Your next step should be forward, for your destination lies ahead.

What Should I Do at the End of My Third Year in College?

The recess between the junior year and senior year in college is crucial, and what you do in this period can have a lasting impact on your future career. You can afford to simply relax during the recess at the end of your freshman and sophomore years—though not a wise idea—but it would be thoughtless or even worse on your part to do nothing during the recess between your junior and senior years. You need to plan carefully and move forward. Making fruitful use of this recess can dramatically improve your chances of getting hired at a good company after graduation or getting admission into a very good program for a master's degree.

Here are a few suggestions that you should seriously consider:

> If you want to start working full-time immediately after graduation, you should pursue an internship in a company of repute or any project that carries value during this recess.

> If you already have an internship by the end of your junior year, you are on track for an exciting future ahead. If you do not have an internship yet and you want to start working full-time immediately upon graduation, you should spare no effort in looking for an internship.

> If, after all your attempts, you fail to get an internship, think of doing some project that will carry value. Talk to any of your college professors about this opportunity.

> If you want to go for a master's degree immediately after completion of your bachelor's degree, you should devote time to studying for examinations, such as the GRE or any other required exam to gain admission. A good score on these standardized tests will put you into the league of people who can get admission into the best schools for pursuing a master's degree.

> Besides doing an internship (should you get one), spend time working on your résumé. You will need a good, well-crafted résumé when you start applying for jobs as you approach graduation. This aspect is often overlooked, and getting a head start in this regard will make your life a lot easier as time progresses.

> Work on personality development, and take courses on these if you can afford it. Primarily focus on developing a confident, pleasing, and presentable manner. You will need to manifest all these qualities when you enter life after graduation. Many people tend to overlook this aspect and do not do anything about it till late in their careers when they find a

need to improve their personality in order to move ahead. You can use this recess to refine your skills and develop into a confident individual who can take on any challenge without hesitation.

➢ Spend some time in preparing yourself for interviews, be they for a job or for admission into a master's degree program. Work on your speech delivery, and get feedback from others to improve your performance. Working on this aspect now will prevent a lot of headaches later.

➢ Also spend time on networking with different individuals. You can use these contacts later on as you look for a job or apply to master's degree programs.

No matter what you do, make sure that the recess between your junior and senior years of college is used productively. You can take some time off and relax for a while, but do not overdo it. How you make use of this time will shape your future career.

The junior year in college is typically the time when people start taking things seriously and change for the better. Your exposure to different subjects as part of your coursework and your interactions with a variety of individuals at this time will mold you into a complete person. Your personality will undergo a sea change, and overall, you will come out of your junior year a much-better person than you were at the beginning of the year. Approach this stage of life with enthusiasm, and do not let any trepidation get in the way of your thinking. Above all, do not be afraid to give shape to your ideas, for only then will you be able to discover your true self.

SENIOR YEAR IN COLLEGE

During your senior year, the coursework is more project oriented. In the junior year, the focus is on teaching you advanced concepts in the field you want to major in, and in the senior year, the focus is on making you understand how the advanced concepts of your coursework are applicable to real-life situations by making you work on projects. At this point, you should feel confident that you have chosen the correct path for achieving your dream career. There may be bumps along the way, but you need only reflect on how far you've come.

The fourth year of college is not only the last year of your bachelor's degree but also the last year of your college life, should you decide not to pursue a master's degree. It is therefore a crucial time for decision making. The decisions you make now can have a lasting impact and can define your life. That does not mean there is no scope for error, but do your best to make rational decisions that are meaningful and can be put into practice.

The first three years of college life are spent gaining knowledge, building relationships, and planning for life after college. The senior year of college is the time to execute your plans and put them into action.

There are big decisions to be made at the beginning of the fourth year. One of the major decisions is to decide whether you want to pursue a master's degree immediately after completing a bachelor's degree or whether you want to take up a full-time job after graduation and then think about doing a master's degree later on. Which career you decide to pursue can have an impact on the decision you make.

For example, if you want to get a master's degree in management or business administration, it would make sense to work in a full-time job for a few years and then pursue the master's degree. In some countries, the universities prefer that the candidates applying for master's degrees in business administration or management have some amount of full-time work experience. On the other hand, if you want to be a medical doctor, it would make sense to continue with your studies and become a doctor before you get into a full-time job. The course of action you need to take will depend on what career path you want to pursue and where you want to live.

If you plan right at the outset of your fourth year in college, you will have plenty of time to make changes should something go wrong. So what decisions do you need to make? Let us find out by looking for answers to the questions that follow:

- Should I pursue a master's degree immediately after my bachelor's degree?

- Should I look for a full-time job immediately after my bachelor's degree?

- What strategy should I adopt to get a good full-time job while still in college?

- How do I harvest the knowledge that I gained in college and reap the dividends?

- How should I network and use it as an investment for the future?

- How do I get organized and plan for the future?

When you have answered all these questions, you will be well on your way to welcoming life with open arms and ready to deal with the challenges that lie ahead. Keep in mind that the answers to these questions will differ for different individuals. You need to find answers that are best applicable to you, for only then will you be able to differentiate yourself from others. If you are able to differentiate yourself and create your own brand, you will be in a position to derive the maximum benefit out of your college education.

Should I Pursue a Master's Degree Immediately after My Bachelor's Degree?

The answer to this question will depend to a large extent on where you live. If you want a master's degree and you live in a country that has a cap on the age of the master's degree applicant, you will have no choice but to pursue it immediately upon completing your bachelor's degree. In such a case, the choice has been taken away from you, and a decision is imposed on you.

However, things are changing rapidly, and in many parts of the world, colleges require that candidates have professional work experience before they apply for a master's degree program. The discipline you want to pursue may also have an impact on your decision.

Here are a few points that you need to consider when deciding on your course of action after completing the bachelor's degree:

> ➤ If the master's degree program that you want to pursue does not stress that applicants should have work experience before applying, then go ahead and complete the master's degree immediately after completing your bachelor's degree.

> ➤ If you are looking to go into a profession where a master's degree or a doctorate is a prerequisite to move ahead, then go for a master's degree

immediately after completing your bachelor's degree. For example, if you want to be a university professor, you will need to have a PhD in order to move up. In such a case, the sooner you complete your academic obligations, the better off you are.

➢ If you want to pursue a career in a highly specialized field, it is more likely than not that you will need a master's degree or an equivalent program to succeed. In such a case, the sooner you get the higher education out of your way, the more advantageous it is to you. For example, if you want to be a medical doctor specializing in fields like cardiology, internal medicine, gastroenterology, psychiatry, neurosurgery, etc., completing the academics as soon as possible will leave you time to focus on your professional career.

➢ Some graduate programs require experienced professionals, and they focus on what an incoming candidate can bring to a program. If you aim to do your master's degree in such a field, you will need to first spend time on the job. For example, in some countries, business schools require that the candidates applying for an MBA program have some work experience, and they discourage candidates from applying when they are fresh out of college with a bachelor's degree.

Whatever the case, ultimately it is you who has to decide the best course of action. If you are intent on getting a master's degree, do so at an opportune time that gives you the maximum benefit, in terms of both financial and intellectual prosperity. The benefits of obtaining a master's degree are plentiful, and should you have the intention of getting a master's degree, pick the timing that offers maximum advantage to you.

Should I Look for a Full-Time Job Immediately after My Bachelor's Degree?

In many cases, it pays to begin a full-time job immediately after completing a bachelor's degree. If your financial situation is precarious and taking a full-time job will ease your difficult situation significantly, it would make sense to take a job. In addition to easing your financial situation, a full-time job in your chosen field will give you much-needed work experience that will help you as you look to advance in your career. Although a master's degree helps you gain specialized knowledge in some areas, a bachelor's degree gives you all the foundation you need to build a great career. Consider the following points to help you decide:

> ➤ If you had to incur a large amount of student-loan debt to finance your bachelor's degree, it may be wise to start working full-time immediately after

college. Once you work for a couple of years, your financial pressures will ease significantly, and the debt burden will get lighter. You can decide on going back to school for your master's degree after working for two or three years. Moreover, when you work full-time and plan well, you will have the added advantage of being able to save for your master's degree.

➢ Besides the financial comfort that a full-time job will offer, entering the workforce gives you the opportunity to rub shoulders with professionals in your field. The experiences you gain as a result of networking are invaluable, and these experiences can help you significantly in your career. The sooner you are exposed to the real world, the more advantageous it will be for you. Of course, a master's degree down the line will further strengthen your credentials, but the work experience immediately after completing the bachelor's degree will help you mature sooner as a professional.

➢ The excitement of earning your own paycheck and benefits via a full-time job and the feeling of accomplishment that follows as a result cannot be matched by anything that academics may offer. Ultimately, the reason for going through the academic rigors is to gain an advantage as a working professional. The sooner you start working after completing your bachelor's degree, the sooner you get to experience the joys that being financially independent can provide.

> If you want to go into a career where the master's degree programs look for experienced applicants, then it would make sense to look for a full-time job immediately after completing a bachelor's degree. Nowadays, many top schools seek master's degree applicants who have good work experience because experienced applicants can enrich a program and make it better. So if you are looking to get a master's degree from a top-ranking school, then go ahead and start working full-time immediately after completing your bachelor's degree. This way, in a few years' time, you can build up all the credentials you need to have a shot at gaining admission.

Besides the financial benefits, working in a full-time job is an enriching experience that allows you to put your knowledge and skills to the test and gain further knowledge in the process. Some of the concepts that you learn in school will start making more sense when you see them applied in real life. Most of the knowledge that lies tucked away at the back of your mind will suddenly find use and come to the forefront.

The whole process can be very exciting, and the sooner you experience this excitement, the more fulfilling your life will be. So if you are the kind of person who wants to experience life firsthand, go ahead and start working immediately upon completing your bachelor's degree. You can then get back to academics and earn a master's degree in due time.

What Strategy Should I Adopt to Get a Good Full-Time Job While Still in College?

Getting a good full-time job is challenging at the best of times, and you need to have a well-crafted strategy to get the job of your choice. You need to think ahead and do your homework before you start looking for a job. Here are a few suggestions that might be helpful in getting the right job after your college graduation:

> ➢ First and foremost, think about the kind of job you want, and then look at the current market situation for these jobs.

> ➢ Talk to career counselors in college, and take their advice as you plan your job search. Ask them if they can give you leads and get you in touch with people who may be able to help you find the right job.

> ➢ Do your own research, and prepare a short list of companies that you would like to target. Begin with an industry search, and then narrow it down to a list of companies within that industry segment.

133

Make sure that your list includes top-tier, middle-tier, and also a few bottom-tier companies in that industry segment.

➤ Once you have a list of companies, upgrade your résumé to make it suitable for the jobs you want to apply for. Get help from the career counselors in your college, and make sure that you take advantage of every available resource when it comes to preparing your résumé. Along with your résumé, create a rough draft of a cover letter that you can submit with your résumé wherever applicable.

➤ Apply online wherever possible. When you apply online, make sure you go to the company's careers website and complete your profile. Most companies prefer that you apply via their careers website rather than e-mailing your résumé to specific individuals in those companies.

➤ Attend career fairs wherever and whenever possible, and talk to the representatives of the companies you are interested in. Besides helping you identify contacts in companies that are on your interests list, career fairs also give you the opportunity to interact with people from many different companies and build up your networking contacts. Many job opportunities show up in career fairs.

➢ If you develop contacts in companies that you are interested in, get in touch with these contacts in addition to applying via these companies' careers websites. Talk to these individuals and tell them about your interests, and someone somewhere will take notice of your candidacy and help you.

➢ Follow up on all job applications submitted, and find out the status from time to time. Do not overdo it, but following up on applications does show that you are a candidate with genuine interest in working for the company.

➢ Be patient, for a job search can be a lengthy and painful process. Accept help from others, but ultimately, it is your effort and perseverance that will get you the job. Be aggressive in your job search, and you will start seeing the results.

Keep applying for jobs, but do so with a sense of purpose. Do not blindly apply. Your aim should be to get *the* job, not *a* job. Make sure that you consider yourself a good fit for the job you are applying for, and then prepare for the interviews. Do not wait for a call before preparing for an interview. Prepare for interviews a little at a time, and that way, you will be ready when the big day finally arrives.

How Do I Harvest the Knowledge That I Gained | in College and Reap Dividends?

Ultimately, your success in your career and in life will depend on how well you utilize the knowledge that you gain in college. Going to college will give you a degree, no doubt, but it is the knowledge you gain while obtaining the degree that will ultimately take you places. A college degree with no knowledge gained can only leave you stagnant. Knowledge does not mean remembering everything you learned in college; it means retaining the fundamental concepts of important topics that can come in handy at opportune moments. It is only when you are able to apply the knowledge you gained in school to real-life situations that you will find success in your endeavors.

Here are a few techniques that should help you utilize your knowledge to your benefit:

➢ Whenever you come across any situation in life, think about the different concepts you learned at school that are related to the issue at hand. Think about the theoretical problems involving these concepts that you might have worked on and how they can be applied to the issue that you face now. Drawing parallels between knowledge gained in class and real-life situations will help you apply your knowledge to practical issues. As you start doing so, you will see your knowledge pay off big time.

➤ When you network with people, make sure that you impress upon them that you are a person who possesses good knowledge. For example, if you go to a career fair and meet with company representatives, talk to them about your interests and how you want to make a career out of your interests. When you drive the conversation in a direction that allows you to display your knowledge, you leave a good impression. When it comes to hiring candidates for jobs, they will have you in mind should you apply. When you talk to people, make sure you grab their interest. But do not overdo it, for you risk leaving them bored.

➤ Pick a project in your senior year that will give you the maximum opportunity to put your knowledge to the test. The more time you spend on such projects, the more you can retain your knowledge, which will help you later on in life.

➤ Never give up any opportunity to showcase your knowledge. During job interviews, make sure you impress upon the interviewer that you possess the knowledge that they are looking for in a candidate. Do not simply answer the questions asked; try to steer the conversation in the direction that allows you to display that you know what you are talking about and that you would be a good fit for the position that you are interviewing for.

Always look for opportunities to put your knowledge and skills to the test. The only way you can make a mark for yourself is when others know that you are the person they can count on to get things done. Do not let any opportunity pass by for lack of interest. Every potential opportunity is a way for you to harvest your knowledge and, in the process, realize your ambitions.

How Should I Network and Use It as an Investment for the Future?

In the business world, networking is a major component of individual success. A seemingly irrelevant individual you met in the distant past at a long-forgotten event may offer you a proposition today that has the potential to change your life. Whether we work for a company or own a company, we are all in effect serving a business, and the better we serve the business the more benefits we will reap. Businesses depend on clients, and anyone you meet anywhere could be a potential client. The importance of networking cannot be overemphasized, and any kind of networking activity that you participate in will serve you as an investment for the future.

Here are a few ways you can network and make sure that your networking experience comes in handy later on:

> ➤ Make sure you retain the contact information of the individuals you meet on special occasions such

as a networking event. Ask them for their business cards or e-mail addresses.

➤ Stay in touch with these contacts once in a while, preferably via e-mail, a less intrusive form of communication. Talk to them over the phone only if they give you express permission to do so, and keep these phone calls to a minimum unless you develop a very close rapport with them. Even when you e-mail them, make sure that you don't do so frequently. People do not like being disturbed frequently, but they do appreciate someone who stays in touch with them.

➤ When you stay in periodic touch with different individuals, you remain in their memory, and if on some occasion in the future you think one of them would be able to help you, you can request that he or she do so. Typically, people try to help if they can, and when they know that you are a good candidate who deserves to be helped, they have no problem doing so. Make sure you also do the same for anyone you are in the position to help. The good deed done by you today will stand you in good stead tomorrow.

➤ If you become an entrepreneur tomorrow, the contacts you develop today could be your future clients or people who help you find clients. In such a case, the more you network, the better your chances will be of flourishing in your endeavor.

Make it a point to develop contacts on all occasions and to retain their contact information. Once you develop a contact, it is up to you to develop and nourish the relationship with the individual. If you do, you will realize the benefits in good time. Never underestimate anyone, for doing so could be like shooting yourself in the foot. A seemingly insignificant individual today could hold the key to your success tomorrow.

How Do I Become Organized and Plan Ahead for the Future?

Planning for the future is a key component of success for anyone. If you do not plan ahead, you stand to lose out on opportunities that may come your way. Opportunities have a way of showing up at the most inopportune moments, and if you are not ready because you have not planned ahead, you could lose out.

Consider the following real-life situation. Two businessmen, Mr. A and Mr. B, both manufacture the same kinds of products, and both of them are looking to expand their client list. Mr. A is a well-organized person who plans ahead and keeps the quotes for his products ready all the time, whereas Mr. B leaves a lot to be desired in that regard. Mr. B's idea of doing business is working only during office hours, so he does not keep any business-related information handy at other times.

Now, both of them attend a party, where they get to meet Ms. C. As they start talking, Mr. A and Mr. B realize that Ms. C is looking to buy the products they make. Ms. C is interested in striking a deal with either of them if they can give her a favorable quote for the products. Mr. A, who is always ready for moments like these, seizes the opportunity and makes a deal, while Mr. B, for lack of proper planning and organization, is left sulking.

The key to success is good planning and being ready at all times. Here are a few points worth considering:

> Always keep your résumé ready, and update it from time to time when you have new accomplishments to add. This saves a lot of hassle. It can be painful to have to build it from scratch when the need arises.

> Even if you land a good job immediately upon graduation, make sure you have a plan of action for the future. Your first job after college is like a stepping stone, and you need to think about how to use this opportunity to move forward in your career.

> If you intend to pursue a master's degree in the future, make a checklist of things you need to accomplish to build your candidacy for a good school. The job you take between your bachelor's and master's degrees is a good opportunity to build your profile. Use your job to take on some challenging projects that will give a boost to your résumé.

➢ Keep abreast of the latest developments in your field, and see how they relate to your interests and abilities. Be prepared mentally to take a shot at any opportunity that might appear on your doorstep.

➢ Always be ready to take on any challenging work or assignment that may come your way or, if need be, to grab any challenging opportunity within reach. When you develop an attitude that allows you to take on challenges, you will always find ways to move ahead in your career, leading to a stable, secure, and prosperous future.

Ultimately, it is in your hands to utilize the knowledge you gain in school to attain your goals and make your college degree count. Being on the lookout for opportunities, and developing a flexible, adaptable nature will be your best future plan.

Always keep an open mind, be receptive to ideas, and be prepared for surprises that may come up from time to time. When you have an open-minded, welcoming attitude toward everything in life, you will be better equipped to handle any situation and find seemingly elusive but not unattainable happiness.

As time passes, you will notice that many things that you have learned at school may change. Just keep in mind, though, that perceptions may change, new ideas may replace the old ones, and technologies may evolve, but the fundamental principles behind the concepts you learned will remain the same. For example, the ideas expressed in the book *The Wealth of Nations*, written by economist Adam Smith in 1776, are as relevant today as they were then, even though economics as a course has evolved over the centuries.

Another much relevant example, also from 1776, is the Declaration of Independence—the document that laid the foundation for modern United States of America. It is as relevant today as it was more than two centuries ago. The concept of freedom has undergone a sea change since then, but the fundamental idea behind human freedom remains the same. This document still finds ample relevance in the workings of the modern-day United States and, as a matter of fact, of most parts of the world.

So welcome change, but keep in mind that as long as you are strong in the fundamental concepts that you have learned in college, you will be well on your way to attaining your personal glory.

You go to college to obtain life-sustaining and life-changing skills. However, it is up to you to use these skills and make everything count. Some people go to college, get a degree, and then start working in a simple job and let all the knowledge and skills they gained in college fade into the background. Don't let that happen to you. The way to differentiate yourself from the rest of your competitors is to use your college education to the optimum extent. Your efforts in college should pay off in the future, or else there is no point in going to college.

There will be ups and downs in life, but anyone with a positive attitude will find more ups than downs. Take pride in your achievement, and make sure that what you gain in college is put to maximum use in your life to obtain maximum benefit. Start doing so, and in no time, you will notice the difference it makes to your life.

CHOOSING BETWEEN A JOB AND A MASTER'S DEGREE

The choice between going for a master's degree and going for a full-time job immediately after completing a bachelor's degree can be a tricky one. In some cases, the decision is pretty straightforward, but more often than not, it can be a challenge to make the right decision.

If you are on the verge of completing your bachelor's degree and obtain a scholarship for a master's degree, there is no need to think. Just go ahead and finish your master's degree, provided you are interested in pursuing advanced studies. Even if you are not interested in a master's degree, forgoing a scholarship when offered one may lead to frustration later on in life, for such opportunities are not easy to come by. You have to decide on your own what to do after completing a bachelor's degree, perhaps in consultation with others. A lot will depend on the career path you want to pursue in laying a solid foundation for your future.

There are several things to consider in making this decision, and the career path that you wish to pursue can play a major part in your decision making. In addition, in some countries, there is an age limit for a master's degree. In such cases, those interested in obtaining a master's degree have a straightforward decision: options are limited, and one has to complete the master's immediately after completing a bachelor's and look for a job after that.

However, in places where there is a lot of flexibility in this regard, a person needs to evaluate all options carefully before making a choice. If you are heavily in debt after completing your bachelor's degree, it might be prudent to work full-time for a while and then think about going for a master's degree. Working for a few years will help you pay off some of your outstanding student loans and at the same time save some money for pursuing a master's. In this way, you are doubly ensured—your debt burden is reduced as you repay your student loan, and you can save to fund your advanced education.

Even if you are in debt, the career you want to pursue will be a big factor in your decision. For example, if your aim is to teach in a college and become a professor, you need to have at least a master's degree, if not a doctorate. In such a scenario, it would make sense for you to pursue your master's and PhD and get them out of the way, allowing you to fully focus on teaching and working toward tenure in a good college or university.

You need to consider several factors before making this decision. Ask yourself the following questions, and see what your answers to these questions tell you:

- If I have incurred a lot of debt to complete my bachelor's degree, what should I do?

- If I have a scholarship available for pursuing a master's degree and I also have an offer letter for a good job, what should I do?

- Would getting a master's degree immediately after completing my bachelor's degree provide a value addition to my career?

- If I want to get the master's degree out of the way before starting my working career, what kind of schools should I consider applying to?

- If I start working full-time after graduating with a bachelor's degree, will I be able to go back and pursue my master's degree?

- If I already have a lucrative job, how will a master's degree help me?

- Will a master's degree help me increase my future prospects?

If you carefully evaluate these questions and find answers that are best applicable to you, you will go a long way in differentiating yourself from your peers and competitors. Once you have answered these questions, you will be in a good position to make a decision as well as prove to yourself and others that you are different.

When you plan for your life, you need to plan in the long term. You do not go to college for short-term benefit; there is always a possibility for betterment of your life. Any decision you make should be one that is relevant for the rest of your life. Let us see how best we can answer these questions in order to find a solution to our dilemma—master's degree or a job?

If I Have Incurred a Lot of Debt to Complete My Bachelor's Degree, What Should I Do?

The answer to this question will depend on the career path you want to pursue. If the amount is high, as is so often the case, it may make sense to work full-time for a few years, get your finances back into a healthy shape, and then return to academics to give impetus for a brighter future. There is a moratorium on the student-loan repayment while you are at college, but the interest does accumulate, and you need to make a careful judgment by looking at the quantity of debt you owe.

Here are a few points you might want to consider before making this decision:

> If the amount of your student-loan debt is very high and you feel that taking a full-time job would alleviate your debt burden and improve your financial situation, then definitely look for a job. If you are interested in pursuing a master's degree later on, make it a point to save some money from every paycheck and set it aside for further education. This way, in addition to lowering your debt burden via a full-time job, you can also avoid going into debt for your master's degree by saving money for it.

> For careers where the pay package is high for candidates with a master's degree and if the master's degree programs leading to these careers do not require that candidates have some work experience before applying, it would make sense to complete the master's degree immediately upon completion of a bachelor's degree. With a high pay package, you are likely to pay off student-loan debt in a timely fashion.

> If you already have a letter of admission from a university for a master's degree program and it comes with an offer of a scholarship or grant (not a loan), you can consider completing your master's degree. The debt already incurred for your

bachelor's degree will not have to be repaid while you are enrolled in school. If you have a scholarship for your master's degree, you can think of working a part-time job during your master's and making payments to reduce your existing student-loan debt burden.

Do not let the burden of student-loan debt bog you down. Although the payments may soon come due, think of the loan as an investment for the future, and make plans as if you had no debt. Only then will you be able to think clearly and make good decisions. The key to not being cowed by student-loan debt is to think of it as an investment that will pay dividends down the line.

If I Have a Scholarship Available for Pursuing a Master's Degree and I Also Have an Offer Letter for a Good Job, What Should I Do?

For those of you who have the luxury of having to make a choice between these two offers, the decision can prove to be a ticklish issue. The best way to approach it is to think long term and not think about what you might or might not forgo in the short term if you choose either one of the offers. It is highly unlikely that anyone will make the decision to forgo both offers. Seen from a long-term perspective, both offers can be used to derive optimal long-term benefits. However, since you have to pick one offer over the other, here are a few ways to look at it:

> If the job offer is from the company of your dreams and it is one that can put you on track to fulfill your long-term career aspirations, then take the job offer. Even though you have to forgo the scholarship offer for your master's degree in this case, your long-term aspirations are better fulfilled by taking the job offer. At a later stage, once you have gained a footing in the company of your dreams, you can return to academics and even ask your company to pay for your master's degree. Even if your company doesn't pay for your education then, you still have a good chance of getting a scholarship for your master's degree with your now much-improved profile.

> If the job offer that you have is not something like a dream come true for you, then it may be wise for you to go for the master's degree with the scholarship offer. This way, you can get your academics out of the way, complete your master's degree, and reenter the job market after that with a much-improved academic profile and with more knowledge and specialized skills than you possessed when you completed your bachelor's degree. The chances of finding a job similar to the one you had to forgo

earlier—or even getting a better one—will be much brighter after completing your master's degree.

➢ If you feel that having a master's degree under your belt before starting your working career will give you an advantage in fulfilling your long-term career aspirations, then accept the scholarship offer and complete the master's degree.

➢ On the other hand, if you feel that getting a master's degree at this juncture of your life will not boost your career and the school that is offering you a scholarship is not the school of your choice, simply take the job offer without any hesitation. You can always come back later on and complete your master's degree.

Both offers may look tempting, but picking one offer over the other will not hurt you much. Just think from a long-term perspective before making a decision. You stand to gain from both offers, and the only question you need to consider in this case is which one will benefit you more over the longer term.

Would Getting a Master's Degree Immediately after Completing My Bachelor's Degree Provide a Value Addition to My Career?

Getting a master's degree at any point of time does add value to your credentials, and the way you market and use your credentials will decide your career progress. However, certain master's degree programs require candidates to have some amount of work experience. Here are a few options for you:

> ➤ If you want to pursue a career for which having a master's degree provides added benefits, then by all means, getting a master's degree immediately upon completing your bachelor's degree is a good option. There are some jobs in the technology and research fields for which the employers prefer candidates who have at least a master's degree, if not a PhD.

> ➤ In case you want to pursue a career in a field where a master's degree only adds value to a candidate who has considerable experience working in the field, then it would make sense to get your master's degree after working for a while upon completion of your bachelor's degree. For example, good business schools typically require their master's degree candidates to have some level of work experience.

➢ If you have graduated with a bachelor's degree from a not-so-highly-ranked school and you want to get a master's degree from a top-ranked school in your field, barring exceptional cases, your chances of being considered for admission for a master's degree in a top-ranked school will only increase if you acquire some quality work experience after completing your bachelor's degree. In such a case, pursuing a master's degree from a not-so-highly-ranked school immediately after completing your bachelor's degree may not provide you with the value addition you seek. It would make sense for you to work for a while after finishing your bachelor's and then have a shot at acquiring a master's from a top-ranked school in your chosen field.

➢ If you are looking for a stable job and are not looking for aggressive career growth, then getting a master's degree immediately after completing your bachelor's degree may not be of much help to you. In such a case, you will do well to get a job after completing your bachelor's degree and see how your interests evolve over time.

➢ If you want to gain entry into a specialized field that requires specialized knowledge, then doing a master's degree in that field immediately upon completion of your bachelor's degree would add a lot of value to your credentials.

When all is said and done, barring special circumstances and depending on the career path you choose, getting a master's degree immediately after completing your bachelor's degree will add significant value to your credentials and to your career. To a large extent, the value added will depend on your ability to market yourself and make use of the skills acquired through your education. You have to work to be noticed and to make others notice the additional value you possess as a result of having a master's degree.

Many people, including managers in some big companies, are ignorant of the value of a master's degree, and you have to differentiate yourself by demonstrating the skills that you acquired through your master's degree.

If I Want to Get the Master's Degree Out of the Way before Starting My Working Career, What Kind of Schools Should I Consider Applying To?

Sometimes, it may make sense to get the academics and college life out of the way before embarking on a working career. In such a case, careful consideration needs to be given to the school that you want to get your master's degree from. If you want the master's degree to unleash its full potential and show you benefits right at the outset of your working career, then you need to think about applying to the top programs in your area of specialization.

There are some top-rated universities whose reputation is such that if you get your degree from one of them, the sheer power of the brand name of the university can land you a good job immediately after graduation. However, different universities specialize in different areas, and it is highly unlikely that one university will be rated number one in all disciplines. You need to find out the top-rated schools for your discipline and make a serious attempt to gain admission to those schools.

That being said, it is not likely that everyone can gain admission in these top schools. A number of factors go toward gaining admission, and a weakness in any one factor can mean a denial of admission. However, that is not the end of the road. A master's degree from any school will have value, and when you get a master's degree from a not-so-highly-rated school, the onus will be on you to gain knowledge, market yourself well, and make a mark.

Here are a few points that will help you decide the kind of schools that you can consider applying to:

> If you have excellent credentials in all regards—such as a high GPA, excellent scores on admission tests, such as the GRE, and very good letters of recommendation from highly regarded individuals—then you should seriously consider applying to the top-ranked programs in your discipline. Given your credentials, your chances of

being admitted to these schools will be very high, and should you be admitted, you can work to derive the full benefit that these schools can offer.

➤ If you have excellent credentials, in addition to applying to top schools, think of applying to a few second-tier schools as a backup plan just in case the competition for admissions in the top schools is extremely high that year.

➤ If your credentials are not so great and you are lacking in certain areas and still want to do a master's degree, think about applying in second- and third-tier schools. Keep in mind that the knowledge you can gain from the third-tier schools is almost the same as you might gain in a top-tier school, and the long-term benefit of getting a master's degree from a third-tier school is almost the same as the benefit derived from getting a master's degree from a top-ranked school.

➤ If you do not have good credentials from your undergraduate degree and want to do a master's degree to improve your credentials, do not worry about not being admitted to any of the top-rated schools. The important thing is that you are on the road to recovery and need to take any opportunity that comes your way. Do not apply to the very top schools; simply focus on gaining admission somewhere.

➢ If money is the deciding factor, then consider the school that is least expensive for you. You can reduce education expenses through a combination of factors, such as scholarships, grants, loans, a significant tuition waiver, or any kind of assistance that lowers your costs. Just pick the school that gives you the maximum benefit or leaves you with the least amount of student-loan debt.

➢ If you have a geographic preference, think about applying to any school in the region of your choice that gives you the opportunity to realize your career goals. In such a case, you alone have to decide what the best option is and which one will help you fulfill your career aspirations.

Although a master's degree from a school with a good name has its own value, that alone should not be your only criterion when considering schools for doing a master's degree. Think about all the factors that will help you realize your goals. First of all, decide what your goals are, and then pick the school that you think offers the best deal for attaining your goals. Once you have the master's degree out of the way, you can focus on unleashing your full potential as you approach your working career.

If I Start Working Full-Time after Graduating with a Bachelor's Degree, Will I Be Able to Go Back and Pursue My Master's Degree?

This is a dilemma that quite a few people face, and it does take a lot of determination on one's part to get back to academics after starting to work full-time. Working full-time helps you bring home the paycheck, and with it come certain privileges that you do not have as a student. Once you get comfortable with life, it is tempting to maintain the status quo and abandon the plans to pursue a master's degree that you made back when you completed your bachelor's degree.

Of course, this is not the case with everyone, and there are many determined individuals who take a break from their working career, return to academics, get a master's degree, and then rejoin the workforce in a better position. These individuals seek more than the comforts that a full-time job brings after completing their bachelor's degrees. Their career aspirations are more ambitious, and they need to get a master's degree to climb higher.

So if you have a bachelor's degree and are employed full-time, ask yourself the following questions:

1. In spite of all the comforts that I have owing to my job, do I have all the tools I need to fulfill my long-term career aspirations and, for that matter, my life's aspirations?

2. Can I get to where I want to in my career in the shortest period of time without a master's degree?

3. Will the bachelor's degree that I already possess be more than enough to attain all my career aspirations when I want to and within the time frame that I have set for myself to achieve these goals?

4. Would going for a master's degree at this juncture be just a waste of time, effort, and money for me? Am I not already on track to attain what I have set out to attain career-wise?

5. Do I possess adequate skills to move up in my career, and do I have the specialized knowledge I need that a master's degree might help me attain?

If the answers to all the above five questions is a yes, then you don't have worry about going for a master's degree. A bachelor's degree is more than enough in your case, and you can simply proceed with your career. A master's degree would be just another achievement that you can showcase on your résumé. If the answer to any one of the above questions is a no, then you need to seriously think about doing a master's degree.

In many careers, possessing a master's degree can hasten career growth, and some companies place a lot of importance on having a master's degree. If you ever feel that not having a master's degree is proving to be an impediment in fulfilling your aspirations within the time frame you have set for yourself, then consider doing a master's degree and treat it as a major project at work whose successful completion will catapult you to the next level.

Once you decide that a master's degree will remove many obstacles from your path, then nothing will stop you from getting it—not even the comforts of life or even your laziness and lethargy toward academics! Ultimately, nothing can come in the way of your goals as long as you set a vision for yourself requiring you to pursue high academic excellence.

If I Already Have a Lucrative Job, How Will a Master's Degree Help Me?

What may seem like a lucrative job now may not appear as rosy down the road as years go by. If you expect that you will feel the same way about your job or career after a considerable time has elapsed, then a master's degree may not make much of a difference in your case.

That being said, it is not easy to predict how we may feel about our life and career in a few years' time. You may have a lucrative job today and get used to the comforts and privileges that come as a result of it. Over time, as you get comfortable with life, your wants and needs may change and grow, and the job that seemed lucrative when you started your career may not be enough to satisfy your growing needs. You may discover that in order to grow, you need a master's degree after all.

Here are a few reasons why a master's degree might help you grow in your career even though you have a lucrative job now:

> Businesses today are a lot more complex than they were a few years ago, and the job categories are more structured, some requiring highly specialized skills. In many job profiles, companies look for candidates who already have advanced knowledge of the concepts involved in those jobs. A master's degree will help you learn specialized skills in certain segments and hasten your career growth.

> Almost all businesses today use complex technology, and running businesses with the aid of these technological advances requires highly specialized skills. Acquiring a position of responsibility in such a scenario may require a candidate to possess advanced knowledge and skills that a master's degree can provide.

> Given the need for specialized skills and knowledge in order to move up the corporate ladder in any industry, having a master's degree can hasten the process of upward mobility in a corporation. Getting a master's degree will help you acquire specialized skills that can open up the route for you to apply for positions of responsibility that command higher pay.

➢ Some companies ask their employees with a bachelor's degree to go ahead and complete a master's degree in order to be promoted to a much-higher level. These companies even fund the education of these employees. More and more companies are putting a lot of emphasis on a master's degree when it comes to promoting employees to a senior level.

➢ There will be a lot of demand for candidates with a master's degree as the job market becomes more and more competitive over the years. The new regulations and complex global economic dynamics are making businesses very complex to operate. Consequently, businesses will require candidates to possess specialized knowledge in their domain, and a master's degree facilitates gaining expertise in specific areas. If you want to reach the executive level, having a master's degree will certainly make the job easier than not having one.

No matter what your career level and no matter how comfortable you are with your job situation, if you get a chance to complete a master's degree, just go ahead and do it. If nothing else, it will stimulate your intellectual curiosity, which in itself will help you move forward as long as you realize the importance of intellect and its proper role in running businesses.

Will a Master's Degree Help Me Increase My Future Prospects?

The answer to this question is yes, provided you make the effort to utilize the full potential of a master's degree. If you just go through the motions, get your master's degree, and do nothing but brag about it, then it is highly unlikely that you will make much progress. A master's degree will give you the skills and knowledge, and you have to make use of this knowledge to prove your worth and make a mark for yourself.

Absent any effort on your part to market yourself and showcase your strengths, you may not realize your true worth or achieve what you are capable of. The onus of making your master's degree count lies on you, and no one is going to hand everything to you on a platter simply because you have a master's degree.

Here are a few points to consider when you have a master's degree:

> ➢ A master's degree provides you with some specialized skills and domain-specific expertise that can help you apply for specialized high-paying jobs.

> ➢ The skill set you possess as a result of your master's degree will help you shop around for jobs and give you the option of picking a job of your choice. If you are not satisfied with your current job situation,

having a master's degree and all the knowledge that it gives you will make it easier for you to change jobs and companies.

➢ When you have a master's degree, do not undersell yourself and apply to any job in desperation, even if your financial situation is dire. Look around for jobs that require highly qualified candidates, and only settle for a good offer. This way, you will be able to come out of your dire financial situation more quickly than you can by underselling yourself. If you are not highly qualified, you will not have this option and have to settle for less.

➢ You always have to think of the knowledge and skills you gained as a result of your master's degree as a long-term investment that is going to pay rich dividends over time. The specialized knowledge that you get as a result of your master's degree will make you a marketable commodity provided you market yourself adequately. The onus is on you to demonstrate that you are worth every dollar a company invests in you when they hire you. A lot of it will depend on how you think and the way you look at things. When you start believing in your abilities, others will start noticing you, and the rewards will follow.

When all is said and done, a master's degree will certainly help you improve your prospects over the long term. If you are looking for a quiet life with a stable job with the bare minimum of necessities, then you may not need a master's degree. But if you want to break into specialized domains and businesses, then a master's degree will certainly prove beneficial.

If you get the chance to pursue a master's degree, go ahead and do it. The choice between a job and master's degree may not be so tricky after all. Think of it this way: you can complete your master's degree in two years or less and then get back to working full-time. In many cases, you may not even have to stop working to complete a master's degree, given the variety of options that are available these days.

If two years of dedication can bring you a lifetime's worth of prosperity both intellectually and financially, it is worthwhile to go ahead and do a master's degree when the opportunity arises. If nothing else, the intellectual wealth that you gain as a result will help you mature quickly, and you will start seeing things in a different light and be different. The more specialized skills you acquire and the greater the domain-specific expertise you gain, the more you will be able to differentiate yourself from your competitors.

8

PURSUING A MASTER'S DEGREE

When you pursue a master's degree, it should be done with every intention of deriving the maximum benefit out of it and making sure that it propels your career in the right direction. Simply getting a master's degree without a plan can have undesired consequences. By enrolling in a master's degree program, you are looking to gain expertise in a few select and specific domains, and gaining this kind of expertise will help you define your career.

By doing a master's degree, you not only try to master a course but also try to master those specialized skills—both academic and otherwise—that give you the confidence to take on the world. In addition, a master's degree involves considerable expense and effort, and none of it should go to waste. If your master's degree is funded by your employer, as is the case in many executive graduate programs, your employer expects you to acquire tools that will help you take on greater responsibility when you complete your education.

On the other hand, if you fund your master's degree either with a student loan or with your own money, you expect to build up an arsenal that will help you recoup your investment and pay rich dividends as well. So it is not only the courses you master that matter but also what your mastery in these courses can help you achieve in future matters. Not only do you need to have a plan for pursuing a master's degree, but also you need a plan while you are pursuing a master's degree in order to help you move forward toward fulfilling your dream.

A master's degree helps you gain domain-specific expertise in the field that you want to build your career in. A bachelor's degree gives you the foundation and some degree of advanced knowledge, whereas a master's degree provides the opportunity to enhance and build on your knowledge so you can put it to use in specialized sectors that require more than the fundamentals.

For example, if you decide to pursue a career in computer software, a bachelor's degree in computers will lay the foundation for you to gain a footing in the software industry, and a master's degree will refine your skills in specific domains, helping you become an expert in a few select fields within the software industry.

Now, who will be paid more, and who can contribute more for an organization—an expert or a worker who has some degree of knowledge? More often than not, it is the expert who gets paid more and can be counted on to troubleshoot whenever a problem arises. Getting a master's degree will train you to be an expert and a troubleshooter—a person who can be relied on to deliver where an ordinary worker may have difficulty. Just going through the coursework and training in a classroom will not make you an expert troubleshooter; you need to do a lot more to refine your skills and gain expertise.

If you begin your master's degree right after completing your bachelor's degree, you can carry the momentum of your bachelor's degree into your master's degree. In this case, you are a student before you start your master's degree and remain a student while pursuing the master's degree. As far as the academics are concerned, you will have no problem, as there is no break in your academic schedule.

One of the big problems you might face in such a scenario is the possibility of getting lost in academics and overlooking the real world that awaits you outside once you finish your studies. The realities of life may come as shock when you finish school if you do not make adequate preparations for life after academia. You need to plan accordingly to ensure a smooth transition from the academic world to the real world.

Most people who begin a master's degree a considerable time after completing a bachelor's degree will be transitioning from a professional job setting into the world of academics. In this case, you may hit a bump on the road and find it difficult not only to adjust to the discipline of an academic setting but also to tune your mind to absorb the academic coursework. You are already grounded in reality, but the extra focus needed to transition into academics may divert you away from the real world and may cause a problem when you leave school. So you too need to have a plan that will keep you on track to achieve the goals you set when you decided to pursue a master's degree.

The basic point is that when you pursue a master's degree, not only do you have to take up the academic challenge but also you need to forge the academic skills gained into a tool that can take you places once you leave college. The last thing you want is to find that you are in the same boat as others without a master's degree and that the effort you put into earning your master's is not bearing the desired fruit.

In order to make a solid plan that will help you unleash the full potential of your master's degree, ask yourself the following questions:

- Why do I need a master's degree?
- Does the school matter in getting a master's degree?
- What kind of schools should I apply to?
- How should I deal with academics?
- How should I build skills that will help me when I leave school?

- How should I convert everything that I learned into a powerful tool that will help me unleash my full potential?

- How do I market myself when I am about to graduate with my master's degree?

Some people come out of a master's degree program without fulfilling what they wanted to achieve. Before they realize it, the one or two years it takes to complete a master's degree are over, and they are left facing the stark reality of the world outside of school. It can take a while to adjust to reality, and the longer it takes, the farther you are from realizing your dream. Do not let this happen to you. Have a plan before you begin your master's degree program, and follow through with it. If you carefully evaluate the above questions and find answers that are best applicable to you, then you will be able to develop the competitive edge that can help you differentiate yourself from others. The last thing you want is to reinvent yourself after completing your master's, so spend some time finding the most suitable answers to these questions.

Why Do I Need a Master's Degree?

Many people with a bachelor's degree intend to pursue and complete a master's degree as well. However, many of these people fail to come up with a satisfactory answer to this question and eventually drop the idea of doing a master's degree. A master's degree carries a lot of advantages, but only when approached and utilized in the proper way. Without a carefully laid-out plan, pursuing a master's degree will only leave you with a hole in your pocket.

Here are a few good reasons why you may consider getting a master's degree:

➢ Some job positions in almost all fields ask for a master's degree, and the pay offered for candidates with a master's degree in these positions is normally higher than the pay offered for candidates without one.

➢ Getting a master's degree gives you domain-specific expertise in some areas, and you can leverage your knowledge to improve your career prospects.

➢ Running any big corporation involves a lot of complex functions, and some of these functions require personnel with a master's degree. You will be categorized among these select personnel if you have a master's, and you can demand to be compensated accordingly.

➢ In addition to all these benefits, monetary and otherwise, a master's degree helps you develop techniques to make efficient and optimal use of your skills. You may still be able to put your skills to the best possible use without a master's degree, but going through a master's program eases the process, and you can attain your career goals sooner with a master's degree than without one.

When all is said and done, a candidate with a master's degree will have considerable advantages over a candidate without one. You can recoup the investment you made in your education sooner with a master's degree. However, the key lies in the way you market yourself. At every juncture, you need to make your master's degree count and show how the knowledge gained via your master's puts you in a position to tackle any challenging assignment.

Does the School Matter in Getting a Master's Degree?

Much as I would like to say no, the answer to this question is yes, it does matter where you get your master's degree from, at least in the short term. Over a longer term, it may not matter much, but in the short term, getting a master's degree from a school of repute will give you a head start. The reputation of some schools gives their graduates a considerable advantage when it comes to getting a good, well-paying job via campus recruitment.

For example, a candidate with an MBA from one of the top five business schools will find it much easier to find a job in the investment banks on Wall Street in New York City than someone with an MBA from a school that is lower down in the rankings. The same holds for other professions as well. There is a way around it, but the path is laden with many challenges.

Here are a few reasons that the school may matter when it comes to getting a master's degree:

> Top-ranked schools in any discipline have a well-connected alumni network that they use to place their graduates into good jobs. The well-placed alumni from top-ranked schools look to fill the open positions in their companies with graduates from their own alma maters. Hence, a person graduating with a master's degree from a top-ranked school can rely on the school's alumni network to find a good job.

> Many big corporations, when it comes to campus recruitment, look to hire candidates from top-ranked schools. They resort to hiring from other schools only when their demand is not completely met by the candidates graduating from the top-ranked schools. A candidate doing a master's degree from a top-ranked school has a considerable advantage in finding a good job with a big company as compared to a candidate graduating from an ordinary not-so-highly-ranked school.

> Top-ranked schools are well funded, and their endowments are considerably larger than those of

other schools. Candidates attending a prestigious school for their master's degree are exposed to a wide array of tools and resources that candidates at an ordinary school may not have access to. This puts the candidates graduating from a reputed school at a significant advantage in the short term. For example, the laboratories and research centers of top schools are far more advanced than those of less prestigious schools.

➢ Having the name of a top school on your résumé puts you at a considerable advantage over your competitors who have not been to a top-ranked school. This specific advantage can give you openings in your career that others may have to struggle a lot for. In many ways, graduating from a top school reduces the effort one has to face in the short term in order to get a footing in the job market.

In spite of all the benefits that the top-ranked schools may offer, it is not possible for everyone to gain admission. We go for a master's degree in order to make a difference in our life over the long term. Short-term benefit should never be the motive for getting a master's degree. If you are prepared to fight it out and struggle a bit initially after graduation, the school from which you get your master's degree will not matter. Although someone graduating with a master's degree from an ordinary school is disadvantaged in the short term, he or she can be at par with or even surpass a graduate from a top-ranked school through hard work, determination, and the ability to use knowledge as a tool to get ahead in life.

What Kind of Schools Should I Apply To?

Given that the candidates graduating from a top-ranked school are at a considerable advantage compared to candidates graduating from an ordinary school, your first focus should be to get admission into a top-ranked school. Of course, this plan may not always work out for a variety of reasons beyond your control. Always keep in mind that the main reason you go to graduate school is to equip yourself with tools and skills that can propel you forward and give you a better quality of life in the future. The primary focus is on gaining knowledge and building your personality, a goal that can be met at any school. So depending on the circumstances, be prepared to go to any school once you have made up your mind to get a master's degree.

Here are few points that you should consider when applying for a master's degree program:

> ➤ If you have preferences about where you want to settle down in the long term and what kind of job you want to get there after graduation, look to apply to programs in that geographic location.

A significant number of companies look to hire candidates predominantly from colleges within their geographic region, so it may not be difficult to find employment in your preferred location after graduation.

➢ If you aim to be the crème de la crème of the people graduating with a master's degree and to land a very good position in a highly reputable company, look to apply to the top-ranking schools in your chosen discipline. Once you graduate from a top-ranked institution, your chances of finding your dream job are much higher than they would be should you graduate from a lower-ranked school in your field.

➢ If you want to go to a top-ranked school but do not have the credentials to get into one, apply to second- and third-tier schools in your chosen discipline as a backup.

➢ Getting into top-ranked schools often depends on factors that are beyond your control. For example, if two people have the same credentials but one has a letter of recommendation from an elite individual, it will be far easier for the one with the recommendation to gain admission to a top-ranked school. The competition for the admission in these schools is extremely rigorous, and the applicant pool is of extremely high caliber. So depending on your background, do your best to get into a top-ranked school, but if that is not an option, pick a school in the next tier. If you are ambitious and driven, you will eventually find a way to compete with candidates graduating from top schools and succeed in your pursuit of making a name for yourself.

➤ If you fail to gain admission into a top-ranked school despite your best efforts, do not be disappointed. Remember, you go for a master's degree to gain knowledge and domain-specific expertise in your chosen field, and your goal is long-term prosperity, not short-term fleeting benefit. So apply to any school where you stand a fairly good chance of being admitted, and plan your career. Over the long term, the effect of the school where you get your master's degree does not matter much. Ambitious and driven individuals can carve out a path for themselves no matter which school they attend. You could be one of them, and when you eventually find success, the satisfaction and feeling of accomplishment that you get as a result will far outweigh anything else. And believe me, the happiness derived from a feeling of accomplishment far outweighs the happiness derived by other means, such as being born into privilege and never having to struggle—and it is happiness that we are all in pursuit of all the time, as long as we are alive and breathing.

Keep in mind that regardless of the school you go to for your master's degree, you can always use the skills gained in the program to help you carve out your own path toward prosperity and happiness. So if you are not admitted to a top-ranked school, simply go to the next best school and build your dreams from there.

How Should I Deal with Academics?

Dealing with the academics in a master's degree program is particularly challenging for those individuals who go back to school after a considerable gap of time since completing their bachelor's degree and for those who join executive programs in which they do their master's degree while working full-time. Individuals who join a master's degree program several years after completing their bachelor's degree will likely transition into academics from a professional working background.

The transition often proves painful. Individuals who opt for the executive programs most likely enroll in a program where the classes are held in the evenings or on weekends. These individuals need to balance their academic schedule with their already hectic work schedules, an act which requires a lot of sacrifices. Those who enroll in a master's degree program immediately upon completing their bachelor's degree typically do not face much of a challenge with academics, for they benefit from continuity of transitioning from one academic program to another.

Here are a few ways that might help ease the challenge of dealing with academics for different individuals:

> Those who are pursuing a master's degree several years after completing a bachelor's degree, especially those who go back to school full-time, need to get focused on academics. Use the discipline and time-management skills that you have learned in your job to deal with your coursework. Besides attending classes, get into the habit of reading books and class notes. It will be difficult at first, but once you start doing it, you will enjoy it. Think of the whole exercise as a professional project that has been entrusted to you, even if you do not find it too interesting. Start thinking of academics as part of your job duties, and proceed. In a period of a month or two, you will notice the difference and enjoy the exercise. Make it a point to involve yourself in classroom discussions, and you will attain the much-needed focus.

> Those of you who have joined an executive program will have your task cut out for you. Not only do you have to attend to your full-time job duties but also you need to deal with academic coursework. Think of the coursework as a challenging work assignment. Set aside time for academics just as you would allocate time when you handle a variety of assignments at work. Moreover, think of the

successful completion of this challenging project as giving you a raise and promotion. In a way, that is the truth, for people go for master's degree via an executive program to move up the corporate ladder. When you start thinking this way and act accordingly, you will find the motivation that will help you focus on academics.

> For those who go into a master's degree program immediately upon completion of a bachelor's degree, think of the one or two years in the master's degree program as a part of your bachelor's degree program that holds bigger challenges. Do not let your spirit slacken. Continue with the same vigor that helped you graduate with a bachelor's degree, and you will find the same motivation that you started with in your bachelor's degree.

> Remember that you started a master's degree to gain knowledge that will help you with your career in the future. Just as you learn things on the job, think of the academics in a master's degree program as a knowledge tool that will help you earn a raise and promotion in your job. When you treat the whole academic venture as a challenging job assignment, the successful completion of which will get you a bonus, you will notice the positive difference that it brings to your mind.

Once you get into the groove of attending classes and studying in a master's degree program, you will find different ways to motivate yourself to do well. Initially, there may be a few hiccups, but approach the whole exercise as a full-time job, and devote a significant part of your day to it. You will see the positive effects in no time.

How Should I Build Skills That Will Help Me When I Leave School?

A master's degree program is about more than getting the degree. It is about acquiring knowledge and skills that will launch your career into a new orbit, and it is also gives you the confidence to face the world and make a mark for yourself. The entire exercise of going through a master's degree program is to gain specialized knowledge in some specific areas that will impart career-enhancing skills, which, in turn, will bring prosperity and happiness to your doorstep. In addition to the knowledge gained, you also need to focus on your personality development via a master's degree program. Since you are in school, it is a good time to identify and work on your weaknesses.

Here are a few skills that you should consider building and improving on while you are enrolled in a master's degree program:

> ➢ First and foremost, work on your known weaknesses, and try to overcome them so that when you leave

school the weaknesses that have plagued you are eliminated.

➤ Place particular emphasis on assignments or projects that you think can have a major impact on your career once you are out of school. For example, if you want to be a manager leading a group of well-qualified professionals, this is a good time to test your management and leadership skills by taking part in group assignments and group projects. Going through the rigors of group work will give you a fairly good idea of where you stand and where you need to improve.

➤ Work on building skills that can help you stand out as an individual and force others to take notice of you. For example, if you want to be a professional who deals with clients and leads negotiations, you must be able to make good presentations. Take on courses and projects that give you the opportunity to build your presentation skills. If you develop into a good presenter, others will recognize this.

➤ In addition to building skills that can help you in your job, focus on building networking skills. Whenever any opportunity arises, go out and meet other professionals, and make it a habit to interact with other well-qualified individuals. This act of networking and the ability to network without inhibition will serve as an investment for the future when you can count on your networks to come in handy.

> Keep an eye on the hottest topics in your curriculum, and make sure you emphasize the latest advances in your field. In an ever-changing business scenario, being up to date with all the latest developments will make you different and put you ahead of others.

In addition to the reasons that made you enroll in a master's degree program, work on any skill that you think will help you differentiate yourself from your competitors in the future. Once you do your own self-evaluation, you will notice some obvious shortcomings you want to work on.

How Should I Convert Everything That I Learned into a Powerful Tool That Will Help Me Unleash My Full Potential?

The chance to make real use of your knowledge will arise once you step out into the real world after completing your master's degree. It is not possible for you to remember everything you learned in school. However, what you can do is to focus on some important concepts and retain them in your mind. The overview of these concepts will help you in the future, not the intricacies underlying these concepts. Once you retain some key concepts, you can always call on your reserves to work on any challenging project that requires knowledge of these concepts.

You can always refer to manuals to work on the intricacies involved behind the key concepts defining the project at hand. Once you are familiar with the key concepts, you will know what source of knowledge to refer to in order to complete a challenging project. On the other hand, if you don't retain the basic concepts in your mind, you will not know how to tackle the project.

Here are few ways you can forge what you have learned into a potent tool that will help you advance in your career:

> ➤ Focus on learning the fundamental concepts and retaining these concepts in your mind. If need be, draw parallels with real-life situations to remember these concepts.

> ➤ Always focus on your final objective, and do not let the nitty-gritty details worry you. Once you have gained a certain amount of knowledge by going through the rigors of a master's degree program, you will have acquired an advanced skill set. Use these skills to help you navigate your way. For example, if you need to work on a challenging project in a job that requires certain advanced skills to begin with, first define and focus on your end goal. Look for a way to navigate to that goal, and as you start working, you will see the way getting clearer.

> ➤ Do not hesitate to use and display your knowledge whenever the situation demands it. For example,

you might be involved in a complex project in your job, and as part of this project, you might meet with the executive management. If you feel that some of the knowledge you gained through your master's degree program will help move the project forward, speak out and let everyone involved know that you have a good idea. Do not hesitate to speak just because the people around you in the meeting are your bosses. Do not wait to be given the opportunity. Seize the opportunity when you see one.

➢ Try to take control of situations when you see chaos all around. Let's say you come across a situation in your workplace in which everyone involved in a project is confused. Even if it does not concern you because you are not part of the project, if you think you have an idea that will help resolve the issue, simply step forward and take charge of the situation. Do not let the opportunity pass you by simply because it does not concern you or because it is not part of your job duties. Acting in a responsible manner will help you get noticed, and your skills thus utilized will help you advance in your career.

The most effective technique of gaining recognition for your skills will be to seize an opportunity without hesitation whenever you sense one. In case you feel no one is noticing you, force others to recognize you by your good acts. Do not try to get attention by acting in a silly manner, for the consequences that will follow are not pleasant. Behave responsibly, blend with others, and develop a helping nature, and—lo and behold—you have the tools to move forward in your career!

How Do I Market Myself When I Am About to Graduate with My Master's Degree?

Marketing yourself is the key to success after completing your master's degree. There are no hard-and-fast rules, but you need to figure out how to make yourself attractive for any prospective employer. Marketing yourself is like adding polish to your skills that will bring you to the attention of someone who is looking to hire the best talent out there.

Here are a few points you should consider:

> If you complete your master's degree immediately after completing your bachelor's degree with no time gap between the two programs, project yourself to a potential employer as an individual who brings a lot more to the table than what they are looking for, as it will help you to get noticed and enhance your chances of getting hired. Typically, big corporations looking to hire candidates with a master's degree look for experienced professionals

and not someone who is fresh out of college. Since in your case you do not have any professional experience to show, you will do well to apply for jobs where the employers are looking to hire candidates with a bachelor's degree. This way, you will have the maximum chance of getting noticed, and if hired, you will also have the opportunity to negotiate a good pay package based on the additional skills that you acquired through your master's degree. However, in this case, you should also be prepared for the risk of being considered overqualified for a job that is looking for a candidate with a bachelor's degree. However, it is a risk worth taking, and more likely than not, you will come out the winner.

➢ If you have considerable work experience along with a master's degree, you have to demonstrate to an employer what it is that makes you an attractive candidate. List the highlights of your professional experience, and further demonstrate how the skills that you gained as a result of your master's degree make you suitable for a position of added responsibilities. Do not simply take whatever job may be offered, but negotiate hard and convince any prospective employer what you deserve.

➢ If you have completed an executive program, the time is ripe for you to talk to your boss about giving you added responsibilities with higher pay to back it up. Ask for challenging projects at work, and demonstrate that you are fit to move up the corporate ladder. Take the initiative by talking to your boss about it rather than waiting to be called at the opportune moment.

You will acquire the skills of marketing yourself over a period of time. Start small, and then get aggressive once you feel confident. Always show a potential employer what makes you an attractive candidate and why you are different from others.

A master's degree will give you the push needed to move up the corporate ladder and to make advances in your career. The results may not be immediate, but as you start to put into practice the skills and knowledge you gained through your master's degree, you will notice the results. Remember, after earning your master's degree, the only way you can add sheen to your credentials is by taking the initiative and demonstrating your skills and putting them to use in real-life situations. The more you do so, the more you will be able to differentiate yourself from others and bring out the uniqueness that defines you.

LOOKING FOR THE FIRST
FULL-TIME JOB

Looking for a job is a full-time job in itself. The more effort you put into this exercise, the better your chances will be of landing the right job. Getting the first full-time job can be a very challenging exercise.

There is one very important thing that you should do before you begin your job search: make sure your phone is set up with voice mail. When recruiters call you and you are not around to take the call, at least they can leave you a voice mail. This piece of information may seem trivial, but believe me, there are people who have lost out on getting interviews because they overlooked this simple aspect. It is rare for a recruiter to call you a second time if they don't get you the first time, especially when they have a large applicant pool to select from.

A job search is more than filling out job applications and hoping for an interview call. You need to do a lot of research beforehand, for the job you end up with could define your future. A good job at the beginning of your career will give you a head start and make your career path relatively smooth. On the other hand, if you end up with a job that leaves you completely dissatisfied, your task becomes a lot more difficult. Not only will you have to endure the bad experience of working in a position you don't like, but also you have to put in extra effort to look for another job.

The longer it takes for you to find the right job, the longer your career progress is delayed. Our careers help us achieve what we want to do in life and make our dreams come true. Not finding the right job only increases the distance between our current situation and our goals, and in such a situation, our vision of our future starts to look like a distant dream.

You may have had some idea of the jobs that you would be eligible for when you enrolled in college and picked your major, but you need to do more research on the job market when you actually start to look for full-time jobs before graduation. Even if you look for an entry-level job when you graduate from college, it is still a good idea to gain as much knowledge as possible about both the job market and the type of jobs you want to apply for.

Recruiters look for candidates who can be developed into business leaders, and possessing good knowledge marks you as a potential leader—one who can be groomed into a good manager. Doing good research on companies before you start looking for a job will help you find the right company and the right job.

Even if you are able to find the right kind of job, it is equally important that you find it in a company that allows you to work in an atmosphere that is to your liking. In many cases, people do get the job they are looking for, but the company culture does not align with their interests.

For example, if you are the kind of person who is full of ideas and wants to make meaningful contributions and you end up in a company where the culture is resistant to change, you will have a very hard time adjusting. In such a case, even if the job is one that interests you and offers good pay, you will not be happy because your ideas may not find any takers. Over time, people get jaded if the company culture does not fit with their personal philosophy.

On the other hand, if you are looking for a steady job where duties are well-defined with no significant changes expected, you will enjoy working in a company where people are resistant to change and happy with the way things are.

In addition to doing research on the job market, spend a considerable amount of time building your profile on paper. Identify what your interests are, what you want to do long term, and what will make you happy. Once you have all these facts ready, you can do research on companies that will give you an opportunity to do what you like.

Looking for a job is not just about completing and submitting job applications. It also involves taking the initiative and reaching out to hiring managers and recruiters. Make it a habit to call up recruiters and explain your situation and interests to them. Talking to recruiters gives you an idea about the current situation in the job market. It is a way to shop around and look for the best deal.

Go to the career services office in your college, and talk to the people there. Often, they provide good counseling and help you make a plan for your job search. They cannot get you a job, but they can introduce you to individuals from different companies, and some of them could be potential hiring managers. If you are completely lost, look for mentors—such as professors or alumni—who can help you in your effort.

When you are ready to look for a job, ask yourself the following questions:

- What are my interests?
- What are my short-term and long-term goals?
- How do I make myself an attractive candidate for a recruiter?
- Where and how do I begin my job search?
- How do I network and build up contacts that can help me in my job search?
- How should I utilize the career fairs?

- How do I find the right kind of companies and approach them?

- Do I need to have a strong backup plan, and what should it be?

- If the job market is very tight, what do I do?

Answering these questions may not get you a job right away, but it will give you an idea where you stand and what you need to do to find the job of your dreams. Keep in mind that looking for a job can often be a frustrating experience, but don't let the disappointments along the way bring your spirits down. Consider your job search an adventurous journey where the ride is often bumpy. Enjoy the journey, but your focus should be on your destination, which, in this case, is finding your dream job. You can make your dreams come true only if you are capable of dreaming.

It is good to be practical and have your feet on the ground, but at the same time, you should have a vision about your future. If you are too grounded in reality and do not dare to dream, then not only will your vision be limited but also your progress will be limited. Dreaming does not mean daydreaming with no action; it means building a vision for a better future and putting your thoughts into motion. Once you have a vision, you can make a plan; once you make a plan, you know what to do; and once you know what to do, your thought leads to action. So be different and dare to dream!

Let's look at the answers to these questions and work to make your dream a reality.

What Are My Interests?

Even though you probably knew your interests when you enrolled in college and chose a major, interests are not limited to the coursework you take in school. Some of the coursework is mandatory to graduate with your chosen major. On the other hand, your interests could expand well beyond the coursework.

Finding a job that encompasses your interests should be your primary aim when you start looking for your first full-time job. The job that you eventually get may not cover all your interests, but making a concerted effort will mean getting a job that significantly caters to them. Answering the following questions will tell you what your interests are:

> ➤ What is it that I love doing so much that it will make me get up early in the morning every day and rush to work full of excitement and enthusiasm?

> ➤ What is it that I love doing so much that it makes my Monday morning the best morning of the week, so much so that on Sunday evenings I think about Monday morning with enthusiasm?

> ➤ What is it that I love doing so much that I will not care how many hours I spend at work?

> ➤ What is it that I love doing so much that at the end of a working day I will still be as enthusiastic as I was when I started the day?

> ➤ What is it that I love doing so much that I will be thankful for the job I have and for reasons other than the paycheck?

> ➤ What is it that I love doing so much that even if I work long hours, I will never notice the time I spend at work each day?

Well, these are just a few questions, and you can pose more to yourself in this regard. However, if you find the answers to these questions, you will know for sure what your interests are and what kind of jobs you would love doing. You may not find a job that is an exact match to the answers to these questions, but if you find a job that is a close-enough match, you will be well on your way to a rewarding career.

It is true that the paycheck is a big motivation for doing a job, but it should not be the only driving criterion. Once you start loving a job and the paycheck is not your biggest reason for working, you can rest assured that you have found a job that aligns with your interests.

What Are My Short-Term and Long-Term Goals?

When you start looking for your first full-time job, you have to think about your short-term and long-term career goals.

The thought of earning a paycheck and being financially independent makes many of us overlook our career goals in the short term. However, overlooking our career goals at the beginning of our careers can have a detrimental effect. People do not want to be in a situation where two or three years into their first job they realize that their career is going nowhere and that they have deviated from their short-term goals.

It is still possible to get back on track, but the effort can be painful. You can avoid all this pain if you think about your goals even before you begin your job hunt and look for jobs accordingly. Job searches can be difficult, but you should maintain your focus and pay attention to your aspirations. The answers to these questions will help you find out your short- and long-term goals:

> ➢ What do I want to do immediately after graduation and in my first job?

> ➢ Where do I see myself in three to five years, or rather, what do I hope to achieve career-wise in three to five years?

> ➢ What are my financial goals for the next few years? What do I want to build for myself within the next five years? Do I want to own a home or any kind of asset within the next few years?

> ➢ In which city do I want to live in for the next five years or more?

- ➢ What kind of jobs and what kind of positions should I be looking for now? How do I want to grow in my job in the short term?

- ➢ What do I want to be in ten years' time, and how do I want my career to evolve over the next decade?

- ➢ What do I have to do to find the right balance between my professional life and private life? What kind of job or jobs will help me achieve all-around comfort?

These are a few sample questions, and you can add your own to this list. Some are tough to answer, but do spare some thought and time for them. The more satisfied you are with your answers, the better you will be at setting your goals. With solid goals in mind, you will have a better chance of finding a job that will make you happy for reasons beyond the paycheck.

Short-term goals should focus on the next three to five years, and long-term goals can span a decade or more. Without goals, you could end up stagnating in a career and just end up working for a paycheck. In such a case, your needs might be met, but you will lead a struggling and unhappy existence. So plan ahead, and know for sure what you want to do before you even start your job search.

How Do I Make Myself an Attractive Candidate for a Recruiter?

The chances of getting a good job and the job of your choice will depend on how well you market yourself. To market yourself well, you need to prepare and transform your candidacy into an attractive package that a recruiter cannot afford to ignore. The starting point for any candidate looking for a job is the résumé, and if you are seeking your first-full time job, you also need to prepare a cover letter that makes a recruiter give your résumé a second look. Many candidates lose out on the chance of getting a good job simply because they overlook the important aspect of marketing themselves well. You need to consider the following points and work on them to make yourself an attractive candidate to a hiring manager:

➤ Work thoroughly on your résumé, and get help from anyone who might be helpful in this regard. The résumé you prepare should command attention. It should present your skills in a manner that catches the eye of a recruiter.

➤ In addition to your résumé, prepare a cover letter that showcases your skills and achievements in a few bulleted points that are easily visible to the reader. If need be, get help from others in preparing your cover letter.

➢ Before you start submitting or circulating your résumé, be sure to listen to the opinions of others who have a good working knowledge of preparing résumés. These could be career counselors in your college or any of your mentors.

➢ Be selective when it comes to applying for jobs. Do not simply circulate your résumé via online job boards where it can be seen by anyone and everyone. If you do, you will get plenty of calls from so-called recruiters whose only interest is in getting their fee from the employer once they place you in a job, without paying the slightest heed to your interests.

➢ Learn the art of introducing yourself and striking up a good, meaningful conversation with a recruiter or hiring manager. Practice this approach with your friends or well-wishers, and the more you work on it, the better you will get. Employers look for candidates who have good people skills and can start and maintain a significant conversation with others. Such skills have the potential of attracting new clients for businesses, so employers look for employees who possess these skills in abundance.

➢ When you meet recruiters, take pride in your skills and achievements, and explain why you think they should consider you as a candidate. However, do not, even for a moment, look arrogant. Be polite, respectful, humble, and assertive where necessary, but get your message across.

➤ If you have the contact information of any hiring manager, reach out via an e-mail or a phone call after you have applied for a job. Follow up on all your job applications, and ask about the status of the position that you applied for. You may not get a response every time, but it won't hurt.

➤ Do not show desperation under any circumstances. Portray yourself as a candidate who knows what he or she wants and will not settle for anything less.

There are plenty of other ways that can help you make yourself an attractive candidate to a hiring manager, but if you start with the points mentioned above, you will be well on your way to finding the right job. The more you absorb and practice the ideas set out in these points, the more efficient you will become in your endeavor.

In your journey toward finding your first full-time job, your job search experience will teach you plenty of things that can make you attractive to any employer, and you can use the lessons learned in your job hunt for your future adventures.

Where and How Do I Begin My Job Search?

These days, you can begin your job search from the confines of your home; all you need is a computer with an Internet connection. Almost all companies have a careers section on their website that provides a way to submit job applications. However, keep in mind that this is just the starting point. Your search does not end in your home. Once you have your résumé, cover letter, and any supporting documents ready, create a list of your interests and what kind of jobs you would love to target based on those interests.

The next step is to look for companies that match your interests and decide on the geographic location where you want to work. Then start applying online.

Here are a few steps that you can follow to ease your job-search process:

➢ Even though you can give your résumé to company representatives whom you meet at career fairs at your college and elsewhere, they will still ask you to apply online via their company website. Make sure you have access to a computer with a good Internet connection, either at home, the public library, a friend's house, or elsewhere.

➢ Once you have decided on the type of jobs you want to apply for, research and prepare a list of companies to target. Also, decide on your geographic preferences.

➢ Allocate a portion of your day for preparing and submitting job applications. During this time, access various companies' websites to complete the online applications.

➢ No matter how long it takes to apply to each position, complete the online questionnaire thoroughly. Do not cut corners in this exercise, or your application could end up in the trash bin.

➢ As you apply for each position, note the important points about the job and the company and any contact information that you can follow up with later on.

➢ Once you have completed a reasonable number of applications over a few days, start contacting anyone you may know who works for those companies, and tell them you've applied. If you have the contact information of the recruiter for any position, call or e-mail and let him or her know about your interest in the position. This may or may not help you, but it will not hurt, and if it works, it could lead to a job.

➢ As you apply for jobs from the confines of your home, try to get in touch with contacts you have established via networking. Depending on the feasibility, go and meet them whenever possible.

Request brief appointments, and if your request is granted, go talk to them and express your interest in the open positions at their companies. As you keep doing this, you will soon find that you have become adept at this exercise. This is also a good way of developing your people skills.

➢ Wherever and whenever possible, try to promote your candidacy for a job with anyone who may matter. Do not be pushy or too aggressive, but express your interest in a docile manner. Many people get jobs this way, and adopting this method of networking can only help your prospects.

In addition to submitting job applications, pursue any means that you think could lead to a job. Do not be too aggressive or pushy in your approach, but never shy away from any potential opportunity to promote your candidacy. Recruiters do not like being pushed, but they admire and appreciate candidates who approach them with genuine interest. Your job search is not restricted to a few specific avenues; pursue any track that you think can get you the job.

How Do I Network and Build Up Contacts That Can Help Me in My Job Search?

While you are in college or anywhere else, you may have the opportunity to develop contacts, one of which could lead you to your first job. Never dismiss any opportunity, never underestimate anyone, and above all, do not assume anything. Besides developing relationships with your classmates, teachers, and other folks at college and elsewhere, use every chance to help you build your contacts network.

Here are a few methods you can adopt:

> Attend every career fair you possibly can. While at a career fair or any similar convention, talk to representatives from different companies, and try to build a rapport. In particular, take their contact information, and follow up with them at every opportune moment.

> Do not impose yourself on any of your network contacts, but stay in touch with them once in a while, preferably via e-mail. Call people only if they give you express permission to do so or if the need of the hour mandates a phone call. E-mail is a less intrusive form of communication than a phone call, but do not flood anyone's inbox with too many e-mails.

> If your contacts are not in a position to help you with your job search, ask them if they can refer you to someone who can. These referrals may not work, but at least it helps you get noticed by others, and sometimes, one of these references might be looking to fill a position with someone like you.

> ➤ Whenever you apply for a job and have the contact information of the recruiter, e-mail or call to reach out to him or her. This is one way of developing networks. Even if you do not get the job, you can reach out again at a later date or whenever the recruiter may have an open position; repeat applicants are often considered for open positions.

There are no hard-and-fast rules for networking. Keep in touch with contacts, and find out if they can assist you in any way with your job search. Just keep in mind that the most seemingly insignificant contact may turn out to be the game changer in a given situation. Networking is an art, and the more you work on networking, the better you will get at it. Just be polite and respectful whenever you approach someone, and you will make a good impression. The job that you finally get may not be the result of your networking activities—most likely it will not be—but networking contacts are your reserve and may serve as a part of your backup plan should all other avenues fail.

How Should I Utilize the Career Fairs?

In addition to direct applications via the websites of different companies, career fairs serve as a good source for finding the right jobs. After all, companies send their representatives to career fairs to look for potential candidates, and many even set up interview shops in a career fair. In several cases, recruiters use career fairs to short-list candidates they can call for interviews later on.

Here are a few ways you can utilize a career fair:

> First and foremost, do not go to a career fair thinking it is a waste of time, for it is not. At the same time, do not have very high expectations either. Think of attending a career fair as going to a place where you can find out whether there are any jobs to your liking and also as a chance for you to promote yourself as a candidate. If nothing else, a career fair may serve as a good place to practice selling yourself as a potential hire. This is also a good place to put your networking skills to the test.

> In addition to finding out what kind of jobs are available on the market, a career fair serves as a place where you can find out if there are jobs that you have not yet considered but might be a good fit. In this case, a career fair serves as a place to widen your vistas and broaden the scope of your job search.

> When you attend a career fair, go to the booths of different companies, and talk to as many people as possible. Present yourself in an amiable and dignified manner, and show interest in what the company representatives have to say to you. When

you give patient attention to their viewpoints, they will treat you as someone who can be considered for any openings.

➤ Often, the people you talk to at a career fair may not have the right job for you, but if you impress them with your presentation, they can refer you to others who might. Many people have gotten jobs via such referrals.

➤ Think of a career fair as a place to practice your interviewing skills. When you talk to the company representatives at a career fair, they will likely have some questions for you. As you answer the questions posed to you, you will get a fairly good idea of where you stand with your interviewing skills. The more you talk to people, the better your interviewing skills will get.

➤ At a career fair, be brief and concise in your speech. Be sure to talk about your skills and accomplishments and why you think you are a good fit for the open positions. Do not bore company representatives with anecdotes that they do not have time to listen to.

➤ At a career fair, do not be in a rush to talk to the company representatives. Be patient, and wait for your turn to speak to them. When you get a chance to talk, do not take up too much time, and be mindful that there may be others in line behind you awaiting their turn. Company representatives notice these subtle behaviors, which will only help you leave a lasting impression.

Although it might seem like a waste of time on occasions, career fairs have their uses. They serve as a good place to find out what kinds of opportunities are out there in the market and also as a place where you can sell yourself as a candidate to any recruiter. So the next time you look for a job, do not hesitate to attend a career fair.

How Do I Find the Right Kind of Companies and Approach Them?

If your first full-time job is the job of your choice, it gives you a great start to your career and a solid footing for pursuing your goals. On the other hand, if you end up with a job that is not to your liking, then you have go through the exercise of a job search again at a later stage and make an attempt to get your foot in the door in the job of your choice.

Rather than go through the painful exercise of looking for another job immediately after starting your first full-time job—one that is not to your liking—it would be wise on your part to put in the extra effort at the very start so you can find the right job in the company of your choice.

Picking the right company can mean a lot for your career. Some companies with openings for the positions that you are looking for may have a company culture that does not align with your personal philosophy. You may not be able to fulfill all your aspirations by taking a job with such companies. You can consider yourself lucky if you get the job of your choice in the company of your choice.

Here are a few ways to identify the right kind of companies for you:

➢ Look for companies that have openings in your line of interest, and get an idea of the pay package for these positions. Good companies typically offer decent compensation and opportunities for career growth. In addition to the pay package, also look at other benefits these companies offer. The type of benefits offered says a lot about the company.

➢ Find out what opportunities for career growth are available in the companies that have job openings to your liking. If getting the right job means having to work in the same position for a long time with no opportunity for career growth, then it is not the right company for someone who is looking to grow and prosper. Such companies may be a good fit for someone who is just looking for a paycheck and does not mind doing the same thing for life.

- ➤ Once you have made a list of companies you like, find out whether they have openings in your preferred geographic region. Unless you are open to relocation anywhere, this aspect can have a significant bearing on your job search.

- ➤ After you have determined everything and arrived at your priority list of companies to which you want to apply, start applying via the careers section of these companies' websites.

- ➤ For a start, the best way to approach these companies is by doing a thorough job with your online application. Take every opportunity to display your talents, and do not cut corners while completing an online application. No matter how long it takes, complete an application with patience, devotion, and dedication. Do not write essay-length answers to the questions posed in the application, but do list your credentials thoroughly.

- ➤ Once you have applied, look for anyone working in these companies whom you can reach out to. Let your contacts there know about your interest in the positions you applied for. As you continue with this exercise, you may end up finding the right contact that can move your application forward.

- ➤ Attend career fairs and see if the companies that you are interested in have sent their representatives.

If you find representatives of the companies that you are interested in at these career fairs, take advantage of the opportunity to talk to them about your candidacy.

➢ At a career fair, even if the company representatives of the companies you are interested in are not relevant to your line of interest, go and talk to them anyway. For example, if you are interested in an operations job in a logistics company and the company representatives of this company at the career fair are from its finance division, do go and talk to them. These company representatives can forward your résumé to the relevant people, letting them know about your interest in the open positions. This kind of networking can help you move in the right direction and eventually lead to a job offer.

First and foremost, do your research, and prepare a list of companies that you are interested in. Make every effort to apply to these companies, and do not spare any effort in reaching out to the powers that be that can influence your candidacy. Job searching is a trial-and-error process, and the secret of success is to keep trying. As you go on trying, it may seem painful, but your efforts will eventually bear fruit. The first delight in a job-search process is not getting the offer letter but getting the interview call. Treat the whole exercise as an adventure, and enjoy it the best you can.

Do I Need to Have a Strong Backup Plan, and What Should It Be?

No matter what you do, the answer to this question is yes. You may not need it all the time, but having a backup plan leaves you with options when the going gets tough. If your job search hits a dead end, you can count on your backup plan to help you move forward.

Here are a few reasons why a backup plan is important:

➢ Having a backup plan will make you feel more confident in your approach since you'll know at the back of your mind that, should things not go according to plan, you have something to fall back upon.

➢ Not having a backup plan can lead to a distressing situation should things go awry. With a job search, if your plan A does not yield any results, not having a plan B can mean developing a new job search strategy from scratch. Now if you have just gone through your plan A, which no doubt has left you exhausted and disheartened, imagine having to build and then execute plan B in such a situation. If you have a plan B handy, you can simply take a small breather and keep moving forward.

➢ A backup plan is like your insurance. Just as we do not expect to meet with accidents when we buy car insurance but have it all the same for contingency purposes, a backup plan will serve as a safety net should things go wrong. When you have car insurance, you can drive confidently, knowing that if something unforeseen happens, you are covered. The same reasoning applies with your backup plan should your job hunt go awry.

Now, in the case of a job search, and in particular when you are looking for your first full-time job, what should your backup plan be? Here are a few ways to prepare a backup plan and put it into action whenever the need arises:

➢ When you begin your job search, in addition to your primary résumé, cover letter, and so on, prepare different versions of your résumé that are suitable for applying in your secondary line of interest should nothing materialize in your first efforts. For example, if you have dual majors—perhaps in finance and insurance, with finance being your core interest—then in addition to preparing a résumé suitable for applying to finance jobs, prepare another one geared toward insurance jobs. This way, if nothing materializes in your primary job search relevant to your interests in finance, you can start applying for insurance jobs. You can also do both together, in which case your backup plan is put into action simultaneously with your primary plan.

➢ Start your job search by applying for jobs in your primary line of interest. If the results are not encouraging, apply for jobs that are not of primary interest to you but are incidental to your core interests. Then if you find a job that is not in line with your core interests, you can still take the job and work your way toward eventually getting into a position that you are really interested in. For example, if you want to make a career in marketing in a big consumer goods company but are not having any luck with your job applications in that regard, you can sidetrack your route and apply for marketing positions in a different kind of industry, such as real estate, banking, or any area where your passion for marketing will be of use. If you end up getting a marketing job in an industry besides consumer goods, you can still apply your marketing knowledge and gain valuable experience before taking another shot in the future at gaining entry into your line of interest (which in this case is a marketing job in the consumer goods industry).

➢ If you are hitting a roadblock at every juncture of your job search, think about changing your geographic preferences. This may often work out if you pick a geographic area that is less competitive and has good opportunities.

Just think of various alternatives that are feasible for you when you begin your job search. You may have an aim, but bring some flexibility to your approach. If you cannot reach your goal by traveling from point A to point B in a straight line, use a circular route to navigate your way to point B. The second route may take you longer, but you will eventually get there.

You must have heard the saying "Better late than never." It applies to everyone, and when things don't go according to plan, having a backup plan will help you reach your destination late. However, you still get to reach your destination, which is better than not getting there at all.

If the Job Market Is Very Tight, What Do I Do?

When you begin your job search, always expect the job market to be very tight. This way, you can be prepared for the worst and plan accordingly. Nowadays, the job market is highly competitive, and getting a good break can be very challenging. However, if you plan ahead and make a concerted effort, your attempts will bear fruit.

Here are few things you need to consider when you encounter a challenging and highly competitive job market:

➢ If you are a highly qualified individual with good credentials, do not undersell yourself, no matter how dire the circumstances. The consequences of underselling yourself are far-reaching and can haunt you for a long time.

➤ If you are in a desperate situation and have to earn some income in order to make ends meet, take up some part-time job as a temporary measure. Devote some portion of your day to looking for a good job. Earning some income to make ends meet will offer you peace of mind to concentrate on your search for a full-time job.

➤ If you are looking for your first full-time job, it is very important to get things right the first time; otherwise, it might take a long time to get back on track and head toward attaining your career goals.

➤ No matter how desperate the situation, do not even consider establishing yourself in companies that do not know how to value qualified personnel. You can accept a job that you do not like, as a short-term measure, but make a concerted effort to look for another job that fits your needs better. It is not worth it to spend much of your career in a company where true worth is never recognized and your potential is not fully utilized.

➤ You must have heard the saying "When the going gets tough, the tough get going." Think of yourself as the tough individual who needs to get going when you are faced with adversity. Take any job that is available to you as a short-term measure of sustaining yourself. However, maintain your focus on achieving your long-term goal. Say you get a job in a small company that is not on your list of favorites and is going through tough times. If you are a focused individual looking to make a difference, you can utilize your ideas and skills to turn around the company's sagging fortunes. Imagine what such a performance can mean to your career! Not only can you turn a situation that was initially not to your liking in your favor, but also you can fulfill your long-term goals by converting that company into one that you like.

> Even though it is not the right fit for you, be grateful to the company that hired you during your time of crisis, and do a good job while you are there. However, focus on your long-term goals, and keep looking for jobs that are a match for your qualifications.

> Take every opportunity to build up and enhance your skills. Never let go of any opportunity that might give you a chance to develop your skills and knowledge.

> If, owing to circumstances, you need to take a job as a temporary measure in a company that does not recognize your true worth, keep looking for

the job of your choice. When you find the right job, exit the company gracefully; only let your displeasure be known if you are treated badly by your employer, but do so in a polite manner without antagonizing anyone.

When you have the resolve and determination, you will find the situation tough only for so long. If you remain persistent in your efforts, you will find that all problems are temporary and eventually discover a way to attain your goals.

Some people treat the job-search process as a big pain and go through the exercise with great distaste. In such a case, the results that follow are not always favorable to the individuals concerned. However, you be different and treat the whole job search exercise as a wonderful adventure. Job searching, especially looking for your first full-time job, can be a painful yet rewarding exercise. The effort that you put into getting a job will teach you a lot and help you become a better person. The experience will leave you enriched and make you a confident individual—one who can find his or her place in the world and be proud of his or her achievements. The only way you can differentiate yourself from your competitors is by identifying your true self and learning to give shape to your interests. Do not settle for anything less than your expectations, and make a mark for yourself by taking the extra step that will take you to your destination.

PREPARING A RÉSUMÉ

In spite of the innumerable articles about résumé writing available and accessible on the Internet, everyone who needs to prepare a résumé has questions. A good résumé is a critical component not only for job searching but also for career development. A good résumé can get you interview calls and help you be noticed in hiring circles. No effort should be spared in preparing this vital document that can take you places.

A résumé is unique for each individual, and everyone needs a good résumé before beginning a job search or looking for career advancement. Now what is a good résumé, and how can a résumé catch a recruiter's attention? Since every résumé is unique, consider any résumé that gets you quality interviews a great résumé. But getting interview calls does not mean there is no need to improve your résumé—there is always room for improvement.

With each passing day, new accomplishments can get added to your repertoire. Life is dynamic and ever changing, and we constantly learn new things. There is always some improvement to be made on your résumé, whether by modifying some of the content or by adding a line to the work-experience section.

Your résumé should mention everything about you that make you a candidate worthy of being hired in the eyes of a hiring manager. However, it should be structured in such a way that the moment someone lays eyes on your résumé, all your strong points and good qualities come to the fore. You must have often heard recruiters saying that the average time a recruiter or a hiring manager spends on your résumé is about ten seconds before deciding whether to toss it or to continue reading it. Now it may be too short a time to make a proper determination, but if the position being filled has received hundreds of applications, it is not unlikely for a recruiter to take no more than ten seconds to filter out résumés that do not meet the job criteria. So if you think that you are qualified for the job that you are applying for, your résumé should show that right at the outset. Do not leave anything to chance, and in particular, when it comes to résumés, do not leave the best for the last.

In addition to the résumé content, it is also very important that a résumé should have a pleasing look. It should not look like a cluster of phrases and sentences all jumbled up together in a congested space. Different sections on the résumé should be adequately spaced out, and those reading your résumé should feel the flow of information that tells them everything they need to know about you.

A résumé that is well structured with all information properly arranged does make your qualification jump off the page. A recruiter will pay special attention to a properly organized and well-formatted résumé before evaluating its content because a neatly presented résumé says a lot about the organizational capability of the individual. Even if you have paid someone to write your résumé professionally, it still goes to show that you are very particular about details and organization. It displays one of your stronger traits, and that can get things moving for you.

A résumé is simply a tool to introduce and market oneself in the job market. It is your way of advertising yourself to a potential bidder. What may be a great résumé for one individual may not be suitable for another, and what may look like a bad résumé on the surface may be the one that gets a candidate the much-needed job. A lot of effort goes into creating a résumé, and it is hard to make a determination whether a résumé is good or bad.

One thing is for certain, however: a résumé that is structured properly and highlights the strengths, credentials, and experiences of an individual in a proper sequence does look appealing, and the candidate is more likely to be short-listed.

Ask yourself these questions, and look for answers as you work to transform yours into a dream résumé:

- What are the different sections of a résumé?

- Should I have a one-page résumé or a multiple-page résumé?

- Should I have multiple versions of my résumé?

- Should my résumé include an objective?

- What should I show in the top section of my résumé?

- Where and how do I display my strengths and credentials in my résumé?

- How do I show my work experience?

- Where do I show my educational qualifications?

- How do I list out the awards, skills, and recognitions that I have earned?

- Where and how do I show the extracurricular activities that I have participated in?

- Do I need a cover letter with my résumé, and if so, how do I present it?

- If the application for a job does not provide any space for a cover letter, how do I make up for the cover letter?

The answers to these questions will vary from one individual to another, and there are no right or wrong answers. Your ultimate goal is to create a résumé that encompasses the answers to these questions and is effective, which, in your case, means getting you a job interview or *the* job interview.

Keep in mind that a résumé provides you with a very good opportunity to differentiate yourself from your competitors. A well-crafted résumé that tells your story in an effective manner can show that you are different from others and that you deserve to be considered for the job. So do not be lethargic while preparing your résumé. Put in your best efforts while crafting your résumé, and let it do the initial talking for you in your job search.

Let us work on the answers to these questions one by one and help prove that you are different.

What Are the Different Sections of a Résumé?

There are no hard-and-fast rules, but it works out best if you can display the information in order of importance based on your objective or what you want the reader of your résumé to see when they look at your résumé.

Typically, a résumé can be broadly divided into the following sections:

Top Section

> *Heading.* This section includes your name and contact information, and it should be at the top of your résumé.

> *Objective.* This section is optional, and it should be added only when you know for sure what kind of jobs you want to apply for.

> *Overall summary and skills.* This section too is optional and is more applicable to experienced candidates as opposed to new college graduates. Add this section only if you feel it will give you a competitive advantage. However, it is not a bad idea to list out some bullet points outlining your competencies and objectives.

> *Key competencies.* This section is optional as well. However, you can use this section to list out some skills in form of key words that stand out and showcase your unique characteristics to a recruiter or hiring manager.

Middle Section

> *Experience.* This is the most important section of your résumé, and all the more so if you are an experienced candidate. This section should list

out your work experience in reverse chronological order. In case of experienced candidates, this section should precede the education section.

➢ *Education.* This section should list out your educational qualifications in reverse chronological order. In case of recent college graduates, this section should precede the experience section.

Bottom Section

➢ *Awards, skills, and recognition.* This section should be used to list out the awards that you have won, the licensures and certifications that you possess, and any kinds of technical skills that you bring to the table.

➢ *Extracurricular activities.* Use this section to list the activities outside of your work that you participated in as well as any related accomplishments.

As I mentioned at the beginning of this section, there is no set format for a résumé, and the above-mentioned sections are just to give you an idea of what a typical résumé can look like. Different people have different opinions about this, and some candidates may need to alter these sections based on their unique circumstances. So do what you think is best for you, and do not worry if you have to change the sequence here and there. However, make sure that the flow of information in your résumé is listed out in the order of importance. The points that you want the reader of your résumé to take notice without fail should be prominently visible right at the outset.

Should I Have a One-Page Résumé or a Multiple-Page Résumé?

It is generally a good idea to have a short résumé that showcases you as a potential candidate for hire. As I mentioned earlier, recruiters spend very little time reading a résumé, and a short résumé makes for an easy read.

Here are a few points that are worth considering when you decide whether to have a one-page résumé or a multiple-page résumé:

> ➢ If you are just out of college, likely you will not have much work experience to show. In such cases, in addition to the coursework you took in college, all you can list on your résumé is any internship or part-time work experience and some interesting projects that you might have worked on in college. It would make sense then to have a one-page résumé. However, if you have accomplishments that cannot be described or listed in one page, do not think twice about having a multiple-page résumé.

➤ It does not matter whether you have a one-page résumé or a multiple-page résumé, but do keep one thing in mind. In the case of a multiple-page résumé, you should list facts about you on the first page that jump off the page. When the first page of your résumé shows items that catch the eye, it is very likely that the reader will want to see what lies on the pages that follow.

➤ When you are just out of college, you are not likely to apply for jobs that ask for experienced candidates. Moreover, it is also unlikely that you will have accomplishments that require several pages to describe. It would therefore make sense for you to keep your résumé limited to one page. You should keep in mind that when you apply for jobs, most applications allow you to provide additional information about yourself that may not be in your résumé. You can list your accomplishments in this space.

➤ For candidates seeking entry-level jobs and looking to get their foot in the door, it makes sense to keep the résumés short, effective, and eye-catching. A one-page résumé with all your qualifications, skills, strengths, and accomplishments listed in a neat fashion can be a very potent tool, one that can get you short-listed as a potential candidate for hire.

> Now if you are further along in your career, the jobs that you have your eye on will most likely require experienced candidates. In such a case, the hiring manager will want to get as much information about you as possible from your résumé, and a one-page résumé may not be enough. As an experienced candidate, you will have plenty of accomplishments, skills, and tools that cannot be described in one page. A multiple-page résumé with everything about you listed in an organized fashion will be much appreciated by potential recruiters.

> You need to understand that a résumé is not a novel that describes the candidate; it is a synopsis that has just enough information to sell the candidate to a recruiter. Even if you need a multiple-page résumé, make sure that everything listed in your résumé makes you marketable and that nothing in it seems redundant.

Generally, you should keep your résumé limited to one page, but if all your qualifications, experiences, and strengths cannot fit onto one page, go ahead and create a multiple-page résumé. No matter what, do not compromise on the appearance of the résumé. If you want to keep your résumé to one page in length, do not do so by using a ridiculously small font size, which will make your résumé hard to read. No recruiter is going to pull out a magnifying glass to read a résumé.

If you have a multiple-page résumé, though, make sure that the first page is a compelling read so that the recruiter will look at the subsequent pages. Also, make sure to maintain the high quality of the content on the first page throughout your résumé. In no circumstances would you want the recruiter to read the first page of your résumé, become interested, move to the next page, and then discard the résumé because the content on the second page is shoddy.

Should I Have Multiple Versions of My résumé?

The best answer for this question is to, first of all, prepare a résumé that tells everything about you and showcases your strengths and qualifications. This résumé is your draft, and everything that you do from now on will revolve around this draft. Time and again, you may need to tweak your résumé based on the job you are applying for. Sometimes, the changes are minor, but other times, you may need to make major alteration. No matter what changes you make, the basic content of your résumé will remain the same; only the manner of its presentation will differ.

When you apply for a job, you first need to look at the job description and then at what the job requires of a candidate. If you think you are qualified for the job, you need to make sure that your résumé gives that impression. To that end, you may have to adjust the way your qualifications, skills, and experiences are highlighted. If the job description stresses a certain skill set, make minor changes to your résumé to highlight the particular skills being sought that you know you possess. The core content remains the same, and the résumé still describes you, but the emphasis shifts.

Here are a few points that can help you decide whether you should have one version or multiple versions of your résumé:

> If you have multiple college degrees in different disciplines or a varied work experience, it is likely that you will be a fit for several different kinds of jobs. As such, it is natural that you will apply for a variety of jobs. Now all these jobs will have different job descriptions and requirements, and you need to tailor your résumé to make it a good fit. In this case, it would be wise for you to have different versions of your résumé to make your task of applying for jobs a lot easier.

> If you think that you are a good fit for different kinds of jobs, it would be prudent on your part to prepare different versions of your résumé—each tailored to a specific type of job—even before you start your job application process. This way, all you need to do is make minor changes to the appropriate version of your résumé when applying for a job rather than doing a résumé overhaul every time.

> If you are very sure about the kinds of jobs that you are going to apply for and they all are in a particular segment of a particular industry, you don't need to have different versions of your résumé. In this case, all you need is one résumé to use it for all your applications. This would work for experienced candidates with great accomplishments to their credit and for ones who are a hot commodity in particular segments of the job market.

> If the job market is tight and good-quality jobs are hard to come by, more likely than not, you will need to have multiple versions of your résumé suited for different kinds of jobs. The more flexible you are, the better your chances of finding the right job, and that means being flexible in creating your résumé. You are better off doing the hard work of creating multiple versions of your résumé before you begin your job search. If you are just out of college, you definitely need to have many versions of your résumé to make your job search easier.

No matter how many versions of your résumé you create, the core content will remain the same, for all these versions are describing and showcasing you. The manner of presentation will differ, with each version highlighting specific aspects of your personality to advertise you and make you marketable.

Should My Résumé Include an Objective?

If you are absolutely sure of what kind of job you are looking for, then you should definitely include an objective in your résumé. In cases where your job search is restricted to a few select kinds of jobs, including an objective provides much-needed clarity to your résumé and does not leave any room for ambiguity. However, if you are not yet sure what types of jobs you want to apply for, preparing a résumé without an objective may not be a bad idea. While a résumé with an objective provides some degree of clarity to a potential recruiter, not having an objective will not hurt. A generic objective as opposed to a more specific one can do the job in some instances.

People who have already established themselves as professionals will typically look to advance in their careers. These people know what they want next and can prepare their résumés accordingly. Their job search is restricted to a few select categories of jobs, all providing career growth. These individuals only apply to jobs to their liking, and if they do not find appropriate jobs on the market, they are willing to wait for the right opportunity to crop up. These individuals will likely include an objective in their résumé, for having one gives additional weight and visibility.

Now, if you are just out of school or about to graduate, it is likely that you have an open mind about your job search. Your first priority is to get a good job rather than look for something specific, since narrowing down your options may make it hard to find a good job. You will need either several versions of your résumé, each with a different objective, or a résumé with no objective.

Preparing several versions of your résumé, each with a different objective, may not be a bad idea and will work in many situations. However, this strategy can have its own limitations and requires that you put a great deal more effort into creating your résumé. For example, let's say you have graduated with dual majors in finance and marketing and are open to jobs in either field. During your job search, you come across a company that has openings in both its finance and marketing divisions, and you are qualified for both. Say you have two versions of your résumé with objectives stating something like this:

> ➤ "A position in finance that gives me…"
> ➤ "A position in marketing that gives me…"

Now, finance and marketing are two diverse fields, and there may be some overlap in certain areas of both, but for all practical purposes, they will be treated as separate fields. In this scenario, it is not enough to have two different versions of your résumé with different objectives, as mentioned above; it is equally important that the contents of the different versions of the résumés match the objectives.

A résumé with an objective stating "A position in finance that gives me…" needs to highlight your strengths that are more suited to finance, whereas a résumé with an objective stating "A position in marketing that gives me…" should highlight your strengths that are more suited to marketing. Not only do you need two versions of your résumé with different objectives, but also you must ensure that their contents correspond to the stated objective. Applying with different versions of your résumé in the same company can lead to a mix-up, which can complicate matters. Of course, some people do it and are successful.

When you are looking for a job, think about the options that will make life easy for you. If you are diligent and thorough in your efforts, apply with different versions of your résumé, each with a specific objective and content matching the stated objective. If you find it too cumbersome, simply prepare a résumé without stating any objective. This option allows you to display all your skills in a single résumé, and you can use this résumé to apply for positions in separate fields.

So there are no hard-and-fast rules about whether to include an objective in your résumé. You can come out with flying colors using either option. Before you prepare your résumé, think about all options, and pick one that seems most sensible to you. If you decide to prepare a résumé with an objective, make sure that the contents of your résumé align with the stated objective. Recruiters and hiring managers look for résumés that are the best fit with the job description, so when you apply for a job, ensure your résumé meets the job requirements, whether it includes a stated objective or not.

What Should I Show in the Top Section of My Résumé?

The topmost portion of your résumé should give your name and contact information. Your name needs to be in bold letters so that the reader knows whose résumé he or she is looking at. If you prefer to be addressed by a name that is different from your given name, you can show that within parentheses. For example, if your name is Annette Browning but you like being called Ann, you can show your name as

ANNETTE BROWNING (Ann)

or

ANNETTE BROWNING "Ann"

or

ANNETTE "Ann" BROWNING

This can come in handy if you have a first name that tends to be difficult to pronounce. It makes it easier for the recruiter who calls you for an interview, as people do not want to mispronounce others' names. People have different views about this, and you need to use your judgment. However, if you decide to show your preferred name on your résumé, make sure that it follows your legal name. Do not use your preferred name or a nickname in place of your legal name.

The next section of your résumé, within the top section of the first or only page, should lay out your objective if you want to include one. Besides the objective, it is a good idea to add a few bullet points offering a summary of your career and skills. This is all the more relevant for an experienced candidate.

For example, something like this right next to your objective or immediately following your name (if you do not give an objective) can catch the eye:

- ➤ Enterprising individual with proven track record of problem solving
- ➤ Go-getter who can be counted on to tackle difficult situations
- ➤ Good negotiator with a track record of building excellent business relationships

These are just a few examples of a career summary that can add value to your résumé. This section is entirely optional, but if you think you have credentials that are worth listing at the top of your résumé, do so by all means.

The next section, which also lies in the top section of the first or only page of your résumé, can vary from individual to individual. If you are an experienced professional, you should list a few of your key competencies. Every job description lists the requirements that the hiring manager is looking for in a candidate. Some of the words in these descriptions stand out and describe the essential attributes an applicant needs to possess in order to qualify for the job. If you happen to possess these attributes, list these qualities in the top section of your résumé. You can devote a small section to your key and core competencies.

For example, this section might look something like this:

KEY COMPETENCIES

Business strategy • Operational excellence • Analysis • Resource allocations • Risk management

Goal setting • Needs assessment • Client acquisition and retention

Communications • Presentations • Streamlining • Negotiations • Consensus building • Problem solving

---

Now, a section like this in the top portion of your résumé definitely jumps off the page. However, this section is more relevant for experienced candidates. If you are just out of college, it is not likely that you will have a proven track record at work that shows you possess these skills. In such a case, unless you can justify your claim, it is better to leave out this section and focus on the next section.

Where and How Do I Display My Strengths and Credentials in My Résumé?

As I mentioned in the above section, if you are an experienced candidate, you should include a section (within the top section of your résumé) that summarizes your career followed by a summary of your core competencies. In addition, you should display your credentials and achievements in every section possible, especially the work-experience section. Highlighting your strengths in the work-experience section does not just mean mentioning your positive attributes; it also means telling how your strengths benefited you and the company you worked for. In short, what did your strengths and credentials help you achieve in your career?

Ultimately, an employer is looking for your ability to use your skills to benefit the organization, not just particular qualifications. When you show that your skills helped you accomplish certain goals in your career, you are providing a potential employer with examples of your achievements. When you provide examples of your accomplishments—

ones that can be substantiated—you become a marketable and an attractive candidate.

In the work-experience section of your résumé, make sure that the descriptions of every role you performed in your work list your achievements and how your achievements helped the company. I will explain this in more detail in the next section:

> If you are an experienced candidate, list your skills in the top section of your résumé, and then show your work experience (in the middle section). Your educational qualifications should follow your work experience, for you are looking for a new job based on your experience rather than just your educational qualifications.

> If you are just out of college with no notable work experience to highlight, what do you think is your biggest strength? Yes, you've got that right: your educational qualifications and your diploma. You have developed certain skills in college by taking some select courses that will have a direct bearing on the career path you choose. So in your case, the section immediately following the objective section (the top section) of your résumé should list your educational qualifications in reverse chronological order. You can add a section for your core competencies in the top section of your résumé

next to the objective and before the educational qualifications section, but it is entirely up to you. If you think listing your competencies as shown above will strengthen your case, do so by all means.

Every section of your résumé will give you the scope and opportunity to display your skills and strengths as relevant to that section. You need to use judgment and show your strengths the way you think will work best for you.

How Do I Show My Work Experience?

This is probably the most important section of your résumé. The way you present your work experience determines your chances of being short-listed for the jobs you apply for. There are different views about how to show your work experience. Some say that a résumé should be as concise as possible, and others say that a résumé should be detailed enough so that the person reading the résumé has a clear picture of the candidate's skills and accomplishments. Based on my experience, I have learned that a very concise résumé can have a detrimental effect in some cases because it may not tell everything about you that you want the recruiter to know. On the other hand, a lengthy and wordy résumé may tell a lot about you, but a recruiter may not have the time and patience to wade through everything.

So I suggest that you take the middle ground and design your résumé in such a way that it tells a lot about you and at the same time is not too wordy. Most people show their work experience using bullet points that just mention what they did in a particular job. This is simply not enough to market yourself and does not help much to differentiate you from other candidates in a competitive job market.

You may have many accomplishments in your job, but if you do not present your achievements in a proper manner, you are doing a great disservice to yourself. Project yourself as an achiever as opposed to just a doer. It is good to be a doer, for a doer is better than a talker, but projecting yourself as a doer may not be enough to help you with your upward career mobility. Let me explain this with an example.

Take a look at this experience section of a well-qualified professional:

- Improved sales performance by working with clients
- Performed monthly analysis of sales
- Implemented new strategies that improved efficiency of sales force

When you read these bulleted points, there is no doubt that this professional is a doer and has some accomplishments to his or her credit, but does this description jump off the page? Most will agree that it may not.

Now, let us redraft this same work experience in a different manner:

- Increased communication with customers, successfully negotiated with existing clients, and added new clients, resulting in a sales boost of 20 percent
- Performed monthly analysis of sales and allocated resources efficiently to improve margins by 5 percent
- Conceived and implemented strategies that motivated the sales team, resulting in improved efficiency of sales force by 25 percent

You can see the difference. The second set of bullet points refers to the same accomplishments listed in the first set, but the second set definitely stands out. The second set of bullet points tells a story rather than just stating some dry facts. The description clearly portrays this person as an achiever—one who means business and can be entrusted with challenging assignments.

So when you describe your work experience, describe it in a manner that shows that you take great pride in what you do. The way you present yourself in your résumé will make you stand out among the multitudes of candidates applying for the same job, and no other section will give you a better opportunity to present your skills and accomplishments than the work experience section. Devote a considerable amount of time to drafting it. Remember, you need to portray yourself as an achiever and not just a doer.

For those of you who are just out of college and do not have work experience to highlight, don't think that you have nothing to show in this section. In fact, you too have plenty to tell about your accomplishments but in a different fashion. In your case, the work-experience section should follow the educational qualifications section of your résumé. You may have done internships or projects that required a lot of hard work. You can definitely think of projects in which you had to work with different teams. All these can be counted as experience that helped you grow as a person, and you should include these experiences in your résumé.

Working on a challenging academic project requires you to work with different individuals, read a variety of study materials, do your own research, make assumptions, challenge yourself, and come up with the final output. You can display these activities in your résumé to show that you are a person who can make a difference. Let me give an example of how this can be done.

The following lines show the work experience of a student who worked as a teaching assistant while at school, completing his master's degree in industrial engineering:

Teaching Assistant, Department of Industrial Engineering

- Conducted undergraduate Engineering Economic Analysis (EEA) and Ergonomic Design (ED) classes

- Helped design, administered, and graded tests and exams in EEA and ED

- Attended classes to keep track of students' attendance and performance through the semester

There is no doubt that the candidate in this case had decent work experience as a teaching assistant.

Now, let us draft this same set of experience in a more effective manner:

Teaching Assistant, Department of Industrial Engineering

- Conducted undergraduate Engineering Economic Analysis (EEA) and Ergonomic Design (ED) classes and helped students understand complex coursework by distilling it into a few concrete examples.

- Good teaching skills resulted in expanded role of assignment. Helped design, administered, and graded tests and exams in EEA and ED.

- Counseled students and guided them, resulting in improvement of the overall class performance.

The same experience, when described in proper details, shows this candidate as a better achiever and as one who can rise to the challenge. It does not matter whether you are an experienced professional or a recent college grad. A good résumé, in either case, is one that shows your work experience in a manner that tells a story and makes it a compelling read. So be prepared to spend a lot of time working on this section of the résumé, and review it multiple times until you are satisfied.

Where Do I Show My Educational Qualifications?

It bears repeating that if you are an experienced professional, the educational qualifications section of your résumé follows the work-experience section. In your case, your education complements your work experience. Simply list out your degrees or diplomas along with the college name or university you graduated from. Do not list out the coursework you took as part of your curriculum. You are using your work experience to market yourself, and you are also stating that you have the education that will help you adapt to new challenges.

If you are a recent college grad with no notable work experience, you are banking on your education to get you a job. So you need to show your educational qualifications in the middle section of your résumé before the work-experience section. In your case, your education is the credential that shows who you are, and this credential makes you a candidate who has a marketable qualification that should be taken seriously.

Besides listing your qualifications, also specify some of the relevant coursework that makes you eligible for the job you are applying for. If you are a recent college grad, you will likely apply for entry-level jobs in your chosen career path. These jobs look not for candidates with experience but for those with the right educational qualifications.

You should describe your educational qualifications in a manner that makes you marketable and shows some of the challenging courses you have taken. Begin the educational-qualifications section by listing the college you last attended, the degree you obtained—along with grades, if applicable—and courses relevant to the job you are applying for.

An example of this section would look something like this:

EDUCATION

ABC UNIVERSITY—Xyz City, State
Bachelor of Science in Physical Sciences   June 2014
Concentration: Physics   GPA 3.90
Relevant Coursework
- Physics
- Atomic Theory
- Organic Chemistry
- Chemistry
- Particle Physics
- Inorganic Chemistry

This is just a sample, and you can work on the design, font, font size, and so on. Highlighting the courses you've taken tells a potential employer about your knowledge. You are making up for your lack of work experience by showcasing the knowledge you possess; you will use this knowledge in your work to accomplish your goals in your future career. Now, if you have more than one college degree, only show the coursework from the most recent college, for it is the most relevant one at this point.

How Do I List the Awards, Skills, and Recognitions That I Have Earned?

The section in which you can show achievements other than your educational and work-related accomplishments will depend on what you want to list. This information should typically be shown in the bottom section of the résumé. Some designations or titles can be displayed alongside your name, and there are stipulated rules mandated by the institutions that award these charters.

For example, charters such as *CFA—Chartered Financial Analyst* and *CPA—Certified Public Accountant* can be displayed after your name in a format specified by the institutes granting these designations. If you are a medical doctor or a postdoctoral scholar who has been awarded a PhD, you can use the title *Dr.* preceding your name. These designations are meant to be used with your name, giving your résumé more weight and increasing the visibility of your candidacy.

When it comes to awards and other forms of recognition, it is not a good idea to display them next to your name in the résumé. These designations should be listed in the bottom section following your educational qualifications or your work-experience section. For example, if you are a recent college grad, your educational-qualifications section precedes your work-experience section in your résumé, and you would show your awards and other designations in a section below the work-experience section. On the other hand, if you are an experienced professional, your work-experience section precedes your educational-qualifications section, and you would show your awards and accomplishments in a section below your educational qualifications section.

The manner in which you list your awards and recognitions can have a significant impact. They can be broadly classified into the following subsections. This section consisting of these subsections can broadly be titled "Awards, skills, and recognition."

It follows the experience and education sections but should lie above the extracurricular-activities section:

> *Licensure.* These are different licenses that are awarded by institutes or regulatory bodies after successful completion of certain courses and

examinations. For example, designations such as *real estate agent*, *insurance agent*, *stockbroker*, and so on allow you to deal in certain trades that you cannot perform without obtaining these licenses.

➤ *Certification.* These are titles or designations granted to you after successful completion of certain courses. They carry weight but are different from licenses in that they may not allow you to perform trades that require separate licensing. For example, if you take some computers courses, you are awarded certificates stating that you are a certified professional in a specific discipline. This title carries weight but is not a substitute for a college degree, nor does it allow you to carry out a trade that requires a license.

➤ *Awards.* These are prizes that you have won in sports or other extracurricular activities such as debating, painting, drama, or acting. You can display these in an awards subsection following the licensure and certification subsections in the bottom section (within the "Awards, skills, and recognition" section) of your résumé. Keep in mind, though, that any awards received due to your performance in a job should be mentioned with that job in the work-experience section. Likewise, if you receive awards for your academic performance in school, mention it with that school in the educational-qualifications section. The awards subsection should list the awards you received outside of your academics and work.

Listing your licensures, certifications, and awards will make you an attractive candidate for a prospective employer. If you have several such achievements to your credit, list all of them, even if it means adding an extra page to your résumé. If something is worth mentioning and you think it will give you an edge over other candidates, go ahead and include it in your résumé.

Where and How Do I Show the Extracurricular Activities That I Have Participated In?

Put all your extracurricular activities in the final section (part of the bottom section) at the end of your résumé. The importance of this section depends on the type of job you apply for. Some jobs put a lot of emphasis on extracurricular activities. For example, if you are looking for a job with a leadership role that requires working with different teams and dealing with both external and internal clients, the hiring manager is certain to look at your extracurricular skills in addition to your job-specific skills.

In such a case, you need to display your extracurricular activities in a manner that draws the attention of the reader. In any case, extracurricular activities provide added weight to your résumé, and some hiring managers put a lot of emphasis on this section. Spend some time developing this section of your résumé, and display it in a way that shows that you are a multifaceted individual who can bring a lot to the table.

No achievement is a small achievement. Do not hesitate to list an achievement or activity that may appear to be insignificant. What may seem unimportant to one person may mean a lot to another. So work on this section with pride. If you are involved in a lot of extracurricular activities, list the ones that have a positive impact on other individuals. Activities that benefit others reveal you as a team player who is ready to help colleagues, and companies look for individuals who possess this quality. This section of your résumé can highlight those talents that the work-experience and education sections of your résumé have not captured.

Extracurricular activities can include a broad range of activities. Here are a few examples, along with a description of how they may be perceived by a hiring manager:

> *Member of a voluntary social service organization.* Participating in these kinds of activities shows that you are a candidate who cares about the broader community and wants to make a difference in others' lives. A hiring manager may see you as a good public relations person who can be counted on to deal effectively with clients and other stakeholders.

➢ *Member of a debating society.* Participating in debates shows that you possess good people skills and can be a good negotiator. A hiring manager may see you as a candidate who can negotiate with tough clients for the company's benefit.

➢ *Dean's list in college.* This shows that you are outstanding in your achievements and have been rewarded by the administration of the college you attended. A hiring manager may see you as a person who can be entrusted with leadership roles and lead projects or teams when the opportunity arises.

These are just a few examples, and you can come up with any number of additional examples based on the extent to which you participated in activities outside of your vocation. Prepare a list after careful evaluation, and pick the activities that stand out for your résumé. List your activities in bullet points or any visually pleasing manner, but make sure not to clutter the last section of your résumé with too much information. A few effective examples are enough.

Do I Need a Cover Letter with My Résumé, and if so, How Do I Present It?

A cover letter gives you the opportunity to introduce yourself and provide a brief summary of your achievements. This is a lot different from a résumé in that here you can address an individual directly, which you cannot do with a résumé. It is always a good idea to have a cover letter to go with your résumé. A well-written cover letter can help you get noticed by the hiring manager, and a compelling one can make a hiring manager review your résumé in detail. If you have an opportunity to interact with a recruiter or hiring manager for any job that you apply for, do so with a cover letter.

A cover letter can be in the form of an e-mail or a hard-copy document that you can submit with your application. If you have the e-mail contact of the hiring manager or a recruiter for a job that you are applying for, you can send an e-mail to the hiring manager after submitting your application. This e-mail is, in effect, your cover letter, where you can mention your interest in the job and provide a brief summary of your achievements that make you qualified for the job.

When you include a cover letter with your résumé or e-mail it after submitting a job application online, make sure you include all the points in the cover letter that make you marketable and attractive. Be bold, and do not hesitate to praise yourself and mention your achievements in the cover letter. Praise can get you noticed.

Cover letters should be short, maybe half a page, and certainly not longer than a page. Even one full page of a cover letter can be long for any recruiter to read. Try to keep it short. Divide your letter into three sections besides the top section containing your contact information.

The first is the introductory section in which you introduce yourself and mention your qualifications and skills. The second section gives your career summary and is the core of your letter. This is where you should mention your significant achievements in four or five short sentences, all in bullet points. Only mention the highlights of your achievements, and do not go into details. Use short but effective sentences that grab the reader's attention. In the last section, mention why you think you are a good fit for the job and that if given the opportunity, you can prove your worth.

Conclude by mentioning that you look forward to hearing back, and thank them in advance for their consideration. It is true that you have not had any interaction when they read your cover letter. So why then are you going to thank them? Well, your thanks at the end of your cover letter will be conveyed to readers only when they read it. So in effect, you are thanking the reader for taking the time and making the effort to read about you. A good, polite introduction followed by a request to consider you as a candidate can often lead to positive consequences, so make every effort to make yourself noticed.

Typically, a good résumé backed up by a well-crafted cover letter can lead to an indication of interest or an interview call. Keep one draft version of a cover letter ready at all times, and make tweaks to it as warranted by the job you are applying for. The basic structure of your cover letter will not change much, for all you are doing in this document is introducing yourself and summarizing your career. At most, you may need to make minor changes now and then.

For example, you may change one of the bullet points mentioning your achievements if you have accomplished something noteworthy since the last time you updated it. Of course, you may need to replace one sentence with another rather than adding a new sentence, as you still want to keep your letter short. When you apply for jobs, look for ways to submit your cover letter along with your résumé, for it adds value to your application process.

If the Application for a Job Does Not Provide Any Space for a Cover Letter, How Do I Make Up for the Cover Letter?

This is typically the case with some online job applications, which often offer no way to attach additional documents. It is not a good idea to add a page to the résumé and include a cover letter there. If you do so, it will most likely be ignored, failing to have the impact that a typical cover letter can generate.

If there is absolutely no provision for including a cover letter with your application, do not fret over it. Simply make sure that your résumé has all the details so that a lack of a cover letter will not diminish the strength of your application. A cover letter is an add-on that can enhance the strength of your résumé by providing an overview of your experience and strengths to the recruiter. But it is your résumé that will help you move forward in the job application process.

Hiring managers at companies whose careers websites do not have any way to attach any additional documents besides your résumé are looking just for candidates' résumés. In these cases, the hiring managers will base their decision just on the strength of the résumés and will likely ignore any cover letter they receive. However, if the online application provides any space for any additional comments, use this space to market yourself. You can add your cover letter here, but it would be a better idea to add a few sentences that describe your outstanding skills. A description of your skills or achievements will tend to be noticed by the hiring manager and will carry more weight than a cover letter in this instance.

The importance of a good résumé cannot be overstressed. Some people think building a résumé is a waste of time and so devote the bare minimum to working on it. Further, some people simply think that just showing a few details of their educational qualifications and work experience on their résumé is good enough to get an interview call. However, you be different and do not consider a résumé as a necessary evil. Invest a significant amount of time in developing your résumé.

Quality time spent on building a marketable résumé can and will take you places. Preparing a good résumé is the precursor to your job search, and having a good résumé handy will definitely make your job search less stressful. The more time, thought, and dedication you put into building your résumé, the better off you will be, for your résumé is a major tool in your arsenal that can help you differentiate yourself from your peers and competitors.

JOB INTERVIEWS

Interviews are a key element in your career development. A good résumé can get you a job interview, but it is the performance in the interview that can get you a good job. Just as you need a good job-search strategy to find the right kind of job, you also need a good strategy to tackle job interviews. Although not a job in itself, preparing for interviews should form a very important part of your career development, and you need to devote considerable time and effort to this exercise.

When it comes to interviewing, as with most things in life, you get good with practice. There will be disappointments on the way, but you should never lose focus. Learn from your interview mistakes, and use them as a guide to perform better in the next one. This is a repetitive process till you finally land the job you desire—your dream job!

So how do you tackle this crucial step of your job search, one that will put you on your chosen career path? You need to have a multipronged strategy to interview successfully. It is always better to overprepare and be ready for whatever questions are thrown at you.

Here are some of the relevant questions you should pose to yourself to get a head start:

- How do I begin my preparation?

- What attire should I wear for the interview?

- What kinds of questions can I anticipate?

- What do I need to do to grab the interviewer's attention right from the beginning of the interview process?

- How do I answer the behavioral questions that I am asked and make a good impression with my answers?

- How do I tackle questions that I don't know the answers to?

- How do I regain my composure if I get lost during the course of an interview?

- How do I prepare myself if I have to face multiple interviewers in the same session?

- How do I leave a lasting impression on the interviewer, something that will more or less assure me of the job?

- What questions should I ask?

- What do I need to do after the interview?

- When and how long after the interview should I follow up, and how should I do it?

Preparing for a job interview is about reinventing yourself. You need to assess everything about yourself and find out what makes you marketable. The process is about discovering who you are and why an employer should hire you. So you need to delve into everything that makes you who you are and how that differentiates you from other candidates. Preparing for and doing well in interviews gives you the scope to prove that you are different from your peers and competitors.

Just keep one thing in mind before you begin your preparation for any interview: no matter what you are asked, all questions in an interview can be interpreted to mean "Why should we hire you?" So all your answers should be geared toward displaying why you should be hired and what makes you a better candidate compared to others applying for the same job.

Many people lose out on the opportunity of getting good jobs because they do not prepare well for interviews. However, you be different and do not forego the chance of getting a good job for lack of interview preparation.

Let us look at the different aspects of your personality by seeking answers to the above questions and, in the process, bring out the qualities that make you different and a candidate worthy of being hired.

How Do I Begin My Preparation?

Even before you begin your preparation, there is one crucial aspect that you need to know before you go to any interview: know your résumé inside and out! You need to know everything you have put on your résumé. If you fail to remember even a minute detail, it could cost you the job. Everything an interviewer asks during your interview will be based on your résumé.

Most often, when you attend a job interview, you are a total stranger to the interviewer. So how will he or she likely begin the conversation after the introductions are over? Typically, interviewers begin by asking you to tell them about yourself. In most cases, this is a "Make it or break it" question. This question gives you the opportunity to advertise yourself and grab the attention of the audience— in this case, the hiring manager. You need to have an answer ready for this, so prepare a short description of yourself.

Keep the following things in mind when you prepare the answer to this question:

> ➢ You should not take more than a minute, or maybe seventy-five seconds, to answer this question. The longer you take, the more likely you are to lose your audience, for you might feed the listener too much information to absorb. Your answer should be brief and simple, but at the same time, it should

tell more than enough about yourself to grab the interviewer's attention. Use five or six sentences in a brief introduction. The key point is to talk slowly but clearly and confidently to reinforce your strengths to the hiring manager.

➢ Do not mention anything that is already on your résumé. Your answer should contain information that cannot fit into your résumé. By the time you reach the interview stage of your job-application process, your résumé will have been read by the recruiter and the hiring manager. They might even have made notes about you before calling you for the interview, and they will have that information readily available. You do not want to sound repetitive, even though you may be speaking with them for the first time.

➢ Start with a sentence about your experience and educational qualifications that make you a fit for the position. Say, for example, you are applying for a job as a software engineer in an information technology company and you have a degree in computer sciences. A good beginning could be, "I have two years of work experience as a database engineer specializing in programming related to inventory tracking and equipment control. My educational qualification of a bachelor's degree in computer sciences concentrating in database management has helped me to acquire skills that are applicable to this position, and…" A sentence like this gives information about two key aspects that define you as a very good fit for the position on offer. One, it tells the hiring manager about your work experience, and two, it outlines how your educational qualification is relevant to the job that you are interviewing for. An answer that begins like this has the potential to grab the interest of the recruiter or hiring manager.

➤ After you have found the ideal introductory sentence to describe yourself, think about what more you need to mention that would give you a head start and an upper hand at the beginning of your interview. Your answer should definitely mention your work ethic—a brief sentence that outlines your integrity and character would be a big plus, telling your potential employer that you can be counted on to deliver in challenging situations.

➤ Talk about how your experience has helped you build certain strengths that are required in this job that you are interviewing for. During your student life or prior work experience, you may have come across situations that helped you gain certain strengths. If these strengths are mentioned in the description for the position you are applying for, include a sentence about your experience that helped you acquire these skills.

➤ Add one sentence that describes you as a person. You could be a person who is a team player, someone who encourages others to bring out the best in them, or someone who is a go-getter. Giving the gist about your personality in one sentence will help the hiring manager determine how fit you are for the position.

➤ In conclusion, add a sentence that mentions why and how your personality, your background, your experience, and your strengths make you a good fit for the position. For example, you could say, "Finally, I would like to add that given my adaptive nature and my experience of handling difficult and trying clients in my previous job, along with my computer skills, make me a good fit for this position."

➤ When you prepare your answers for possible interview questions, make sure you prepare them in simple language. Refrain from using words that do not form a part of your normal speech. Make sure that you practice your speech a lot before you go for the interview. Not preparing well may make your answers sound artificial, and your speech may sound memorized, which does not leave a good impression. Unless the position that you are applying for requires you to have good language skills, keep your answers and language as simple as possible.

To summarize, you need to prepare a small paragraph describing yourself that is no longer than five or six short sentences and can be recited in little over a minute. This introductory statement about you should contain the following sentences:

1. A sentence about how your education and work experience make you the right fit for the job you are interviewing for

2. A sentence about your work ethic

3. A sentence about your strengths

4. A sentence defining your personality

5. A sentence that mentions why you are a good fit for this job

You may add another sentence or two if you think it will strengthen your case. You have to use judgment about what will make you marketable and what might weigh the balance of the scales in your favor over other competitors. Always remember, you know yourself best and are the best judge of yourself. So the introductory statement should be prepared by you. You can get help from others, but the essence of this statement must come from you.

On the surface, it may seem a simple task, but preparing a paragraph about you is not so easy. As you work through it, you will realize that you have to go through several iterations before you arrive at a final statement that you find satisfactory.

Now, preparing this introductory statement describing you is by no means the end of your interview preparation. It is just the beginning!

You will need to prepare answers to plenty of questions. You can find examples of many generic and not-so-generic interview questions from a variety of sources. Do your own research, and prepare a list of possible questions, and then prepare the answers to those questions. Once you have your answers ready, practice answering the questions as you would with a real interviewer. If need be, simulate an interview situation by asking someone to ask you questions and answering them as you would in the interview. Practicing for interviews is a painful exercise, but the more you do it, the better you will get at it, and the more confident you will be when you face the real interviewer for a real job.

What Attire Should I Wear for the Interview?

An interview is not just about determining what you can do or what you know; it is also about determining who you are. Knowing who you are tells others about your personality, your professionalism, and all that is likable about you.

Now, when it comes to judging an individual's personality in a very short time, the appearance of the person being interviewed is given a lot of importance. Appearance, in this case, does not mean the looks of the individual; it's how the individual carries himself or herself.

Good attire makes a huge difference. When you interview, you are in a professional setting and need to reflect your best professional demeanor. It is absolutely essential that you also dress in professional attire. Make sure you look up the latest professional-attire trends and dress accordingly. In case you are not sure, err on the side of conservatism, for it is better to be overdressed than underdressed for an interview.

Now, no one expects you to be dressed in expensive clothing. Just make sure that your clothes are neat and clean and fit you well. Your attire should not make you feel uncomfortable. It should aid your personality and not get in the way of it. Dress professionally, be proud and confident, and go with the flow.

What Kinds of Questions Can I Anticipate?

When you begin your preparation, you will find scores and scores of questions that are all potential interview questions that you should be prepared for. Does that mean that you have to spend months preparing for your interview? The good news is that as you dig deeper into these possible interview questions, the more you will find that the answers to most revolve around finding answers to the questions listed below. In the final analysis, all you are trying to do is sell yourself to the interviewer and get the job. In essence, you have to describe yourself in the interview in a way that makes you an eligible candidate.

Now, in order to market yourself, all you have to do is prepare a sales pitch. When you think hard, you will notice that you need to find answers to the following questions, and they are all about you:

➢ What can I do?

➢ What are my strengths?

➢ What are my likes and dislikes?

➢ What are my interests?

➢ What do I enjoy doing most?

➢ What motivates me?

➢ What are my weaknesses?

➢ What have I done, and what more do I need to do to overcome my weaknesses?

➢ How can I improve?

➢ What have I gained from my education?

➢ What has my work experience taught me?

In addition, you need to find answers to the following questions that are more relevant to the kind of jobs you are looking for and your desired the career path:

> How does my background make me a fit for the jobs that I am applying for?

> Am I a good team player or a good independent worker?

> What can I contribute to the role that I am applying for?

> What incremental value can I bring to the company that hires me?

> What distinguishes me from others, and how can I differentiate myself from candidates applying for the same job?

> How will the knowledge that I have gained over the years help me in the job that I am applying for?

> What are my career aspirations, and how do I plan to go about pursuing them?

These are a few of the questions, but if you make an attempt to find the answers, you will see that the responses to these questions can serve as a response to many others. So rather than compiling a very long list of questions, all you need to do is find answers to a few questions that describe you and your eligibility for the jobs you are applying for.

When you prepare and review your answers for the questions above, you will notice that you feel a lot more confident than you were when you began compiling the questions. The answers tell you a lot about yourself and form a good foundation for answers to other possible interview questions. The key is to lay a solid foundation and build on that.

What Do I Need to Do to Grab the Interviewer's Attention Right from the Beginning of the Interview Process?

There are some precursors to the interview before the actual conversation starts. A crucial part of the interview process is to arrive early but not too early. If you arrive a few minutes early, you will have time to compose your thoughts. When you have regained your focus after reaching your destination, you are more calm and self-assured. Now you can concentrate and think of a good way of introducing yourself to the interviewer.

The very first step is when you face your interviewer for the first time. First, they welcome you, and you introduce yourself. You can do a lot to grab the interviewer's attention during these initial exchanges. Start by introducing yourself and giving a confident handshake. After this comes a crucial but often overlooked element of interviewing that can help make the right impression: thank the interviewer for calling you for the interview and for giving you the opportunity. More often than not, it leaves a good impression, one that you can carry through with you during the interview.

By no means is this initial step a deal clincher, but it does set you on the right track. When you attend an interview, you are initially nervous and trying to collect your thoughts and compose yourself. You may have it in your mind to thank the interviewer for giving you the opportunity, but the words may not form in your mouth. So keep this in mind, and prepare your nerves accordingly.

You will often notice that a good introduction raises your confidence level. Sometimes, interviewers engage in pleasantries before the start of the interview. This is your opportunity to make an impression. If you make intelligent conversation during this phase, you will grab the interviewer's attention at the very outset. If you are nervous and at a loss for words, you may find that even after the interviewer has spoken several sentences, you are still tongue-tied. Not only that, but you may even have a hard time following what the interviewer is saying. You may consider practicing this step with some of your friends or family members. It may feel awkward when you practice, but it does help you gain confidence.

When you interview, you are in a professional setting, and the interviewer too wants to maintain his or her best professional demeanor. So one thing you know for sure is that you will not experience any hostility. Keeping this in mind, if you proceed accordingly and remain professional, you can leave a lasting impression. Once the initial introductions go well, you can approach the interview confidently.

How Do I Answer the Behavioral Questions That I Am Asked and Make a Good Impression with My Answers?

A key component of any interview process is a set of behavioral questions. These questions help the interviewer assess you as a candidate and how you will fit into the grand scheme of things. There is no right or wrong answer to these questions, but a good response is crucial to getting the job.

As you do your research and compile your list, you will find that there are plenty of behavioral questions and other follow-up questions that combine some basic behavioral questions. Do you go about preparing answers to hundreds of questions? Even if you do, will you be able to remember the answers to all the questions? Above all, is that an effective strategy?

While it may seem like a good idea to prepare answers to as many questions as you can, it may not be the most efficient way to prepare for an interview. When you prepare answers to many questions, you will gain a lot in knowledge, but you may still omit some crucial components, which may prove detrimental later on. Keep in mind that any behavioral question thrown at you during an interview is asking you to describe yourself and how you may be a good fit for the job.

So all these answers, in this context, pertain to you, and you need to find answers that are applicable to you. Some questions may not be relevant to you directly, but you still need to find a context in which you have encountered such a situation. The best way to prepare for these behavioral questions is to prepare a list of incidents from your past experience that challenged you and brought out the best in you.

If you are applying for your first job after college, you may not have any significant work-related incidents that you can include in an answer to a behavioral question. You may have some experience working part-time, and if you have any noteworthy experiences, by all means mention them. However, in your case, it is a good idea to mention challenging projects that you may have undertaken while at school. Think of incidents that demonstrate your ability to work in groups, your leadership qualities, and your strength, personality, and character. Think of a few incidents, and try to relate them to different behavioral questions.

Now if you are an experienced professional who is looking for a new job, it is likely that you have experienced challenging circumstances that tested your resolve and determination. Write down a paragraph or two about these incidents first, mentioning what you learned from these incidents or how you applied your knowledge and experience to overcome a challenging situation. Also mention how your ideas helped with the situation and the eventual outcome.

Then look at the list of behavioral questions and see how the incidents that you have listed relate to these questions. You will be amazed how one incident can be used to answer several different questions, and you can relate the same incident to highlight different aspects of your strengths, knowledge, skills, and overall personality.

For example, say you handled a project at work in which you had to lead a team and make tough decisions while handling a complex assignment with a set deadline. This project can serve as an example to demonstrate your leadership qualities, decision-making ability, and capability to meet deadlines effectively and efficiently. So now your task is greatly simplified. Instead of compiling a long list of behavioral questions and answering them one by one, all you have to do is write down a few noteworthy incidents from your experience and relate them to the different possible questions that you may be asked during an interview.

During a single interview session, it is highly unlikely that you will be asked more than a handful of behavioral questions. Now given the time constraints of an interview, you may not be able to mention all your past experiences to the interviewer. Just make sure that you have answered the questions properly and narrated incidents from your past that substantiate your claim.

For most jobs, you will have to face more than one interviewer in separate sessions, and some questions will be repeated. In such situations, you can mention incidents to the second or third interviewer that you have not mentioned to the first. This way, you can tell a lot about yourself. When a company makes a decision about hiring a candidate, the different interviewers generally compare their notes and then come to a conclusion. When you mention various incidents to different interviewers in your responses to behavioral questions, you give them a lot of information about you that will help them make a decision.

Remember, when preparing answers to possible behavioral questions, you do not have to make up stories. If you dig into your past, you will find plenty of incidents that can be used to substantiate your claim. Just devote some time to it. You may not have captured a criminal on the most-wanted list nor won a major contest, but you will still have accomplishments that are worth cherishing.

Just think of situations that gave you a feeling of accomplishment. Often, simple accomplishments get a job done. So try not to set a benchmark that may make you look down on yourself. Take pride in your accomplishments, however insignificant they may seem, and use them to substantiate your claims as you go about preparing answers to behavioral interview questions.

Good answers will help you justify your claim that you are the right candidate for the job. When you look back, you will notice that there are many small achievements in your past that made you really happy. It is time now to narrate these incidents to lay your claim to the job you desire!

How Do I Tackle Questions That I Don't Know the Answers To?

Often, in interviews, the interviewer will ask a follow-up question based on your answer to a previous question. One answer leads to another question and so on until you find that you don't know the answer to the question being asked. This is nothing unusual and can happen to anyone. There may be situations during an interview in which you find that you don't have a good answer to a question.

The first thing you need to do is try to absorb the question. If it is not clear, politely ask the interviewer to repeat the question or be more specific about what is being asked. Do not think even for a moment that it is not acceptable to ask an interviewer to clarify or repeat a question. It is perfectly all right to do so. In fact, in some situations, it gives the impression that you have a good grasp of things and that you want clarification so you can give the right answer. As the interviewer repeats the question, it will give you time to absorb the information being asked for and to align your thoughts and regain your composure.

As you listen carefully, you can form your train of thought and prepare an answer in your mind. Once the interviewer has repeated the question and clarified it, you can then begin to answer. This exercise of asking the interviewer to repeat the question thus gives you some valuable time to nudge your memory and orchestrate your answer.

Now there may be situations in which the question is like a bolt from the blue and you have absolutely no idea what it is about. In such circumstances, you can politely say that you don't have the answer to the question. However, keep in mind that the manner in which you say that you don't know the answer can have a positive impact. If you bluntly say, "I don't know," it will have a negative impact. If you say, "I am sorry, but I haven't come across such a situation before," it might have a positive impact. Imagine for a moment that you are the interviewer. Which reply, in your opinion, sounds more pleasing? I bet you will say it is the second one.

If it is a behavioral question that asks you to describe a specific situation you have encountered but it does not apply to you, you can simply say, "I am sorry, but I have not faced that type of situation before, as my role did not call for any such activity." If the question that left you stumped is testing your knowledge about any specific topic, you can say, "I am sorry, but I have never come across this topic."

It is not necessary that you know the answers to every question asked in order to get the job. What the employer looks for in most cases is how you would fit in to the role and to their company culture. So you may not know everything about the role, but you may still be a good fit if you qualify on many other grounds. Some activities are job specific, and you learn them only when you have worked in that particular role. Moreover, the same role may require working with different sets of systems in different companies. So the functions of a role may vary from company to company. If you are a good fit overall, you may still get the job without knowing the answers to every question.

So don't be rattled if you do not know the answer to a question. You still stand a chance, so focus on your next question. If you don't know the answer and it is the last question of the interview, do not despair. Typically, before concluding the interview, the interviewer asks if you have any questions for them. You can use this opportunity to ask some good questions and share your opinion to leave a good impression. All is not lost if you do not know the answers to some questions; you can still make a good case for yourself that can get you hired.

How Do I Regain My Composure if I Get Lost During the Course of an Interview?

This can happen at any time during an interview, and even very experienced candidates may find themselves in such a situation. It often happens that you are not satisfied with your answer to the question being asked. You then try to explain and clarify what you just said, but the right words don't come, and you get stuck. As you try harder, the situation gets messy, and you are trapped in a vicious loop—you want to clarify yourself to come out of the messy situation, but the more you try to clarify yourself, the messier it gets. You are at a loss to find the right words, and you even find it difficult to form correct sentences. You start losing your composure, and your body starts to sweat. What do you do, and how do you get yourself out of this situation without incurring any damage?

The answer, my friends, lies in your mind. You need to block your mind from thinking about the answer you have just given—the one that you are highly dissatisfied with. Just try to forget it, and block your thoughts for a moment or two. Now look for a fresh start and a new beginning. Prepare your mind for the next question. Take a deep breath, but do not appear to be nervous. Compose your thoughts, and don't feel embarrassed. The interviewer is a human being and has, no doubt, also encountered ticklish and embarrassing situations. He or she will certainly understand your fiasco and may not judge you outright.

When you start thinking this way, positive thoughts come to your mind, and pretty soon, you will regain your composure. Treat the next question following your crisis as if it is the first question in your interview, and answer calmly. When you do so, your answer will be very satisfactory. Now one satisfactory answer leads to another, and within a couple of minutes, you will be back at your best. The situation that seemed out of control just moments ago is now completely in your grasp, and you will feel as if the unpleasant situation is a distant memory from the past. As you practice answering potential interview questions, you will gain confidence and can avoid unpleasant situations.

When you start feeling that you are losing your composure, pause for a moment and shoot a question to the interviewer to clarify that you've understood each other. You can ask, "Is this the detail you are looking for?" or, "Have I explained myself clearly?" Questions such as these give you a few precious moments to regain your composure.

The interviewer will then take some time to answer your question. As he or she answers your question, try to assess his or her facial expression for an indication about which course of action to take. If the interviewer appears unperturbed by your dilemma, you know you can still continue the way you are going and make amends as needed. If he or she appears confused with your dilemma, you can recompose your thoughts while listening to the interviewer's response and make the right move when you start answering again.

The key is to relax and gain time to overcome your nervousness. Even a few seconds of breathing space can be enough to put you back on track in such circumstances. Rest assured that these actions on your part will not be construed in the wrong way. The interviewer will perfectly understand any concern you may have.

How Do I Prepare Myself if I Have to Face Multiple Interviewers in the Same Session?

It is not uncommon for companies to conduct what is called a panel interview in which a small group interviews the candidate in a single session. The idea of being interviewed by multiple people at the same time may seem intimidating. Do not fear, my friends, for handling such interviews may not be as difficult a task as it might seem. Remember, whether you are being interviewed by one person or a panel, you can only be asked one question at a time. So focus more on the question than on the group. Your answer will remain the same whether the question is posed by someone on a panel or by an individual conducting the interview alone.

There are few points worth mentioning that you should keep in mind when you attend a panel interview:

> ➢ One person in the panel will ask a question at a time, and you need to make eye contact with the person who is asking you the question. Do not look at others when someone is asking you a question.

> ➢ When you begin answering the question posed by one member of the panel, look at the person who asked you the question. After a couple of seconds, turn your gaze to another member of the panel. As you continue with your answer, make sure you have looked at everyone, one after the other, without

gazing at any one person for a long time. As you move your gaze from one person to the other, do not turn your head too fast. If the answer to the question is brief, it is all right if you are not able to meet everyone's gaze in the panel by the time you finish your answer.

➢ Make sure you make eye contact with each one. It may seem intimidating in an interview setting to make eye contact with everyone on the panel, for each member of the panel may have a different facial expression during the course of the interview. However, as you start to make eye contact— even reluctantly—with the members, you will immediately notice that you are gaining confidence.

➢ Do not think of the panel as a monster out to scare you. Think of the panel as a group of friendly people who are trying their best to make you feel comfortable.

➢ Do not judge any member in the panel by his or her facial expression. Many times, you will find out to your surprise that the person who appears to be very serious is the most jovial person you have ever met.

➢ Absorb the question in your mind, ponder it for a moment, and then begin answering. Often, you may find that one member asks you a question and as you are about to answer, another member poses a follow-up question. In such cases, absorb both questions, and answer them one by one.

➤ Often one member asks a question and, after you have finished answering the question, the follow-up question comes from another member. So be prepared to go back and forth among the members as questions keep coming.

It is a good idea to practice for a panel interview. Invite friends to pose as panel members and ask you questions. When you have practiced this way, you will feel very confident during the real interview.

How Do I Leave a Lasting Impression on the Interviewer, Something That Will More or Less Assure Me of the Job?

The key to this is the manner in which you answer the questions. It is not enough to answer the questions correctly; it is just as important to maintain a good demeanor during the interview. If you are polite and answer the questions with humility and in a dignified manner, you will leave a lasting positive impression.

Bring out your best behavior when you are attending an interview. That does not mean that you leave your good manners in the interview room when you step out if it. It is always important to be professional and polite at all times. However, politeness is crucial during an interview because you are being tested for some qualities, your manners among them.

Maintaining your dignity, exhibiting a pleasant demeanor, and appearing to be friendly, jovial, and enthusiastic about the job on offer will add a new dimension to your answers. The interviewer will see you in a new light and judge accordingly. You can appear self-assured and confident and fully in control of the situation. However, do not be arrogant or appear to be so. Even if the interviewer is trying to test your patience, do not exhibit any negative trait that can work against you.

Suppose the job you are applying for requires the candidate to have a lot of patience, such as a teacher. It may not be uncommon for the interviewer to ask questions in a way that tests your nerves. The interviewer, in this case, is just trying to find out if you are a good fit for the job. When faced with such a situation, remain calm and answer the questions as professionally as possible. Do not display any impatience. Even if the same question is asked several times during the interview, answer the question as if you are being asked the question for the very first time.

Besides your demeanor and correct answers to the questions, your approach to answering the questions in an interview can make a lasting impact on the interviewer. When you are asked a question, listen attentively; take a moment or two to digest the question, and then answer. You don't have to raise your voice much, but do make sure that whatever you are saying is clear and audible. If you do not understand the question, ask the interviewer to clarify or repeat the question. If you want to know if the answer you have given is the one the interviewer is looking for, ask if he or she wants any further detail or an example to substantiate your answer. All these small elements add up and improve your chances of getting hired.

One of the most crucial components of an interview is to make sure you don't say anything negative. Never ever say anything negative about anyone or anything. A small negative statement is enough to ruin your chances even if the rest of your interview turns out to be far above your expectations. Do not, under any circumstances, criticize your previous employer, and do not say you didn't like your prior jobs. Even if you had unpleasant experiences in the past, do not say anything negative about them.

When asked about any unpleasant experience, mention the challenges you faced in overcoming the situation, and explain what you learned from the incident. You can also mention how that incident helped you become stronger and a better person. Being positive about every situation tells the interviewer that you are loyal to your employer, you are not critical, and you are open to challenges. There are incidents in our lives that we would rather forget and ones that make us angry when we think about them.

There are situations when your previous manager may have treated you badly. However, you should take them all in stride and find out what positives you gained. For example, a bad experience teaches you what to avoid in the future, and that in itself is a positive outcome. Keep this in mind when attending an interview, and answer the questions accordingly.

The overall personality that you display during an interview says a lot about you to the interviewer. If you exhibit a pleasant and confident demeanor during an interview, it makes the interviewer think you will be an asset to the company if hired. He or she will see you as someone who will not disappoint under any circumstances. Keep this in mind when you go for an interview, and you will come out with flying colors.

What Questions Should I Ask?

Before concluding any interview, the candidate is given the opportunity to ask questions. It is not uncommon for the interviewer to allow the candidate to ask questions during the interview itself. So come prepared to ask questions. Don't simply say, "I don't have any questions." That makes a very poor impression. Questions are your opportunity to further demonstrate to the interviewer that you are really interested in the job and the company. When you ask good questions, you come across as being able to carry on an intelligent conversation, and companies look for such people. The questions you ask should be relevant to the job you are applying for and to the company as a whole.

Before the interview, do your own research and note some points about the company. If your research is thorough, it will lead to some excellent questions for which you may not have the answers. Some of the questions can be job specific, and others can relate to the company in general. Prepare a list of a few questions that would address any concerns you might have. The interview is a good time to address these concerns, as this will help you make a decision about the job.

Sometimes, you may find that your concerns are not properly addressed by the interviewer, in which case you may think twice about your prospects in the company should you eventually get hired. If the interviewer is able to address your concerns, it might reinforce your conviction about the company and the future you might have there.

Good questions are typically job or company specific. You can ask about the company culture in general and what it expects from a new employee. You can also ask how it evaluates new employees and what the long-term prospects for a new employee are. The more you study the company before the interview, the better you will come across as a candidate who is genuinely interested in the job.

For the most part, avoid asking about the salary being offered for the position. Based on your research, you may have a fairly good idea about the pay scale for the position, but many companies do not include their pay scale in the job description. Unless you are asked about your salary expectations, do not bring up the topic of pay. Companies typically expect good candidates to know what they are walking into and to have done some good research before attending the interview. You will get your chance to negotiate the salary when you get the offer of employment. Until then, if salary is not mentioned, let it remain a pleasant mystery.

Good questions from the candidate often lead to an intelligent conversation between the hiring manager and the candidate. This conversation gives candidates the opportunity to reinforce their claim about their eligibility for the position.

What Do I Need to Do after the Interview?

Immediately after the interview, as you are on your way off the company premises, thank the interviewer for giving you the opportunity. Even though you may have thanked the interviewer for the very same thing right at the beginning of the interview, do it again as you are about to leave. Besides thanking the interviewer, mention that you had a pleasant time and that you are very interested in the position. State that you look forward to hearing back from the interviewer.

In case he or she has not already given one to you, ask for the interviewer's business card. Should he or she not have one readily available, ask for an e-mail address or phone number or both. It is very important that you at least get the interviewer's e-mail address, for that leaves open the channel for future communication without being too intrusive. You may also ask how long it might be before you can expect to hear back from the company.

Once the interview process is over, send an e-mail to everyone you interviewed with. In your e-mail, thank them for giving you the opportunity to talk with them, and mention that you enjoyed the time you spent with them. The thank-you e-mail is also your opportunity to mention any relevant facts about you that you think will strengthen your case. Keep the e-mail brief, for it is highly unlikely that the hiring manager will have time to read a long e-mail from a prospective candidate. If you are very eager to hear back from him or her, say so in the e-mail.

Once you have completed this formality, it is time to wait for the good news. Do not be impatient or fret too much in case of a delay. At the same time, no matter how hopeful you are, do not wait too long for a job offer. Some companies take a long time to make a decision, so do not think that a long delay is a bad sign. Many companies do let you know of their decision even if it goes against you. However, be prepared not to hear anything; for reasons unknown, some companies never make any effort to follow up with rejected candidates. So if you experience an inordinate delay after the interview, just look for other opportunities. Your job search is not over till you have an offer letter or have started work in your new job.

When and How Long After the Interview Should I Follow Up, and How Should I Do It?

Do not expect to hear back anything for at least a week or two after the interview. It is a very trying time, and it is easy to get impatient. Do not let your impatience get the better of you or take any irrational step. Some companies can take up to a month to decide. If you do not hear back anything after fifteen days, you can reach out to the hiring manager or other contacts to find out whether any decision has been made.

The first step is to e-mail the hiring manager, not call, for e-mail is a less intrusive form of communication. If you get a response to your e-mail informing you of the status, you can relax. If you do not receive any response to your e-mail, you can follow it up with another e-mail. During the fourth week, or maybe a month after the interview, you may call your company contacts and find out whether the position has been filled.

Now if the hiring manager has specifically mentioned that it is all right to contact him or her anytime, you can get in touch a week after the interview. Moreover, if the hiring manager has indicated how long it might take to reach a decision and that time period has elapsed, you can initiate contact via e-mail. You are anxious to know the result and move on, but you should be cautious and not let your impatience ruin your chances.

Some companies do not have the courtesy to inform rejected candidates of their decision. In such cases, no matter how hard you try to communicate, you will never get any response. The e-mails go unanswered, and the phone calls always go to voice mail. You can leave a message, but you are unlikely to ever get a response. The bright side of such a scenario is that you know now for sure that you do not want to work for such a company. If they do not show the basic courtesy, you are better off looking for greener pastures.

The questions mentioned in this chapter are by no means a comprehensive package that will take care of your interview needs. The interview process is a trial-and-error effort, and as you put in the effort, you will learn new things all the time. However, these questions and your answers to them will set you on the right track if you are completely lost and are in need of guidance.

As you make an attempt to answer these questions and start your interview preparation, you will notice that you are gaining not only in knowledge but also in confidence. Therein you will find the path and your eventual destination. Job interviews offer you the best opportunity to show to the interviewer that you are different from other candidates and how these differences make you a better candidate for the job in question. Some people take interviews very casually and go unprepared, and what follows in such situations is not pleasant. Do not let this happen to you. Do everything you can to help you master this crucial step to put your career in top gear.

PLAN TO TACKLE STUDENT LOANS

Repayment of student loans takes up a large portion of a person's income after college even if he or she finds decent employment upon graduation. The longer it takes to find a job, the more the debt keeps mounting, for the interest accrued is added to the principal. Student-loan debt is a major cause of worry for many people at the very start of adult life, and it continues to be a source of worry for many long after their college days are over. If you have a student-loan debt, you need to put a careful strategy in place to prevent the debt from growing out of bounds and keep this monster in check!

It is more painful to part with your money to pay off student-loan debt than it is to pay for any other kind of debt. Granted, our student loans give us college degrees or diplomas that we will use to find employment and better our lives. However, unlike other debts, such as mortgages or car loans, we don't get to see any tangible benefit of student loans in the near future. Even for those who are lucky enough to land a cushy, well-paying job immediately after graduation, paying off student loans can hurt, for many see it as money going down the drain for no visible benefit. When you take out a mortgage, you own a home, which gives you a great sense of pride. When you take out an auto loan and buy a car, you get to enjoy the drive every day. In the case of a student loan, you don't see any gratification or asset.

You, as an individual with a student-loan debt, need to focus on repayment. First of all, think what it is that you set out to achieve when you made the decision to go to college by incurring debt. Yes, you went to college to get the degree that will provide you with long-term benefits if it is used as a powerful tool. Although you wish that you had no student-loan debt, you need to think that this debt helped you attain something valuable (higher education), which, if used wisely, will pay rich dividends over time. Now, when you start thinking this way, the next step is to focus on what you need to do in order to fulfill this obligation of student-loan repayment while enjoying life to the fullest.

So how do we go about paying off student loan without letting it pinch us too much? The solution lies in finding answers to several questions that we need to ask ourselves. Before going into those questions, I would like you to keep one thing in mind all the time, and that is to think positive and not let negative doubts consume your mind. No matter how dire your circumstances, don't ever think that you will not be able to pay off your student loan. Negative thoughts like this one serve as a strong deterrent to progress and finding the eventual happiness that we all seek.

Don't even think of your student loan as a debt! Think of it as an asset that is going to give you delayed gratification at some point in the future. Think of it as an investment that is going to pay you dividends. Now, converting this debt into an asset requires answers to the following questions. Keep in mind that the answers will vary from person to person, but a careful evaluation will prove to be of immense help as you venture out into life after college.

Here are the following questions:

- What do I need to do to feel that my student-loan debt is an asset and not a liability?

- What is my total effective debt, including the interest paid over the term of my loan, and how do I tackle it?

- What is the estimated time frame over which I should repay my student-loan debt?

- What kind of repayment plan should I opt for?

- What percentage of my income should I devote to repaying my student loan?

- What kind of jobs should I be targeting in both the short and medium terms to help me pay off my loan?

- In case of adversities, what backup plan should I have to make my student loan payments?

- How do I balance my student-loan repayment with the repayment of other debts that I might incur in the course of my life?

It is always better to think about the answers to these questions even before your repayment period begins. However, it is never too late, even if you have to look back and reevaluate your repayment strategy. The answers are just as relevant to an individual facing a midlife financial crisis because of a student-loan default as they are to a student who is about to enter the job market after graduation. The strategy should always be a long-term one rather than a short-term one or one generated on the fly. Also, remember that the manner in which you interpret and find answers to these questions will differentiate you from your peers and competitors.

Do not be one of those who look at their outstanding student loan with regret and get bogged down in their endeavors when they think of making monthly loan payments. Think of making the monthly student-loan payments as an investment—one that will reap dividends in future—and concentrate on the benefits that you will derive over time owing to your decision to take a student loan and gain invaluable education.

What Do I Need to Do to Feel That My Student Loan Is an Asset and Not a Liability?

Your student loan is an asset; at the very least, it is an investment that will pay off in the long term, and the payoff you receive far outweighs the income and benefits you would have generated without it. There is a huge psychological barrier that prevents you from thinking this way, and once you can overcome this frame of mind—one that makes you regard your student loan as your worst liability—you will reap the full benefits of your student loan.

You attend college or another institution of higher education because you expect to derive some skills that will help you live a better-quality life. It is to progress toward this higher echelon of society that you incur a student-loan debt. Going to college and incurring a student-loan debt is a way to work to better your situation in life. That means that when you incur a student-loan debt, you are in a way thinking of it as a long-term investment—something that will stand you in good stead and help you attain your goals in life. Why, then, should you think of it as a liability when it is time to repay this loan? It is true that you have to forgo a certain portion of your paycheck to pay off the debt, but thinking of it as an investment will help numb the pinch of forgoing a fraction of your paycheck to meet this obligation.

While you don't see any immediate tangible benefit from a student loan, as you might with a mortgage or a vehicle loan, neither do you see immediate tangible benefits from so many other things in life that you spend money on. Say you get your paycheck on a Friday afternoon and go to a pub in the evening and get drunk. What is the outcome? You might get temporary gratification out of your intoxication, but what do you end up with the following morning? Apart from a hangover, you are in for a far bigger shock—and that is when you notice that the money in your account has dwindled.

In most cases, you do not think of this incident as a loss-making venture; instead, you think of it as something that helped you have fun. Now, would you really consider a few hours of fun at considerable expense a tangible benefit? If you do, you are in for bigger shocks in your life at the most unexpected and inopportune times.

So isn't your student loan repayment a far better proposition than this "fun" incident? It is, for in addition to giving you a valuable qualification in the form of a diploma, it has helped you attain and equip yourself with skills that will help you in life. These skills will come in handy at different points as you work your way up in society. Above all, your education gives you self-respect, a feeling of accomplishment and pride—and all this was possible because of your student loan.

No matter what you lose in life, no one can ever take away your accomplishment and the satisfaction you derived as a result of it—your education and diploma! Long after their college days are over, people still look back with a feeling of pride and joy. So, is your student loan not an asset? Is the repayment of your student loan not an investment in your betterment and an effort to attain a higher purpose in life?

If you make full use of your skills, you will attain great heights and gain back at least ten times the amount you invested in your student loan. So take pride in your achievements—the very first of them being your education—and navigate your way toward a better future. Always think of your long-term goal, and move on ahead.

What Is My Total Effective Debt, Including the Interest Paid Over the Term of My Loan, and How Do I Tackle It?

By the time you are out of college, the accrued interest added to the original amount borrowed leaves your outstanding debt significantly higher than what you initially borrowed. Although most of us are aware that the loan is compounded with interest, we tend to overlook this fact until it is time to start repayment. Of course, knowing this early on may not make much of a difference, as there is very little anyone can do to make payments on a student loan while still in school. The money you earn as a student by doing part-time jobs is seldom enough to cover student-loan payments. And if you make enough to cover your tuition and living expenses while at school, you will not incur the student-loan debt in the first place.

Now look at the interest owed over the life of the loan, and add that amount to the outstanding principal balance. That, in effect, is your total debt, for that is the total amount you will repay over the life of the loan. It is better to take this view when it comes to looking at the outstanding debt, for it gives you the true picture of how much of your future earnings you will forfeit to repay your loan.

Bear in mind that the total outstanding-interest amount over the life of the loan will be known with accuracy only if your loan is a fixed-rate loan. If you have a variable-rate loan, talk to the lender or look at your contract terms, and find out under what circumstances or when the interest rate will change. The change in interest rate can be good news or bad news. The variable interest rate can at times go down, which will lower your monthly payment, but it can also go up, which will raise your monthly payment.

In the case of a variable-rate loan, look at all possible scenarios, and prepare a repayment schedule based on each one. The extreme cases are either that for an extended period of time the interest rate remains very high or that it remains low. In the first case, your monthly payments will be high for a long time, and in the second case, your monthly payments will be low for a significant portion of your loan term. You can work out the repayment schedules for both of these extreme scenarios on an assumed interest rate and take the middle ground, which would be the average of these two extremes.

Depending on the time and energy you wish to devote to this exercise, you can evaluate several repayment scenarios based on different interest rates and take the average of these scenarios to assess how much interest you will likely owe over the life of your loan. For all the scenarios mentioned above, just do a straight calculation of the interest owed in dollar terms without considering discount rates or the time value of money. You can choose to do more complex calculations, but it may not be worth the effort.

The next step is to make a plan to repay it. It is obvious that you will need an income to pay off the loan, but good planning will give you an idea of what you need to do to pay it off without feeling the pinch. Always remember that you went to school, incurred a debt, and earned a degree because you expect something in return. You did not go to school to be left debt-ridden and broke for the rest of your life. Now that you have gained an education, it is time to make it count.

The first step is to get a job, which we have discussed in earlier chapters. Of course, your first job after college may not pay much, but your pay will increase as you gain experience and navigate your way through the job market and life. Depending on the salary you make in your first job, you will know what fraction of your paycheck you can put toward servicing your student-loan debt.

If you make enough to make the payments as outlined in the initial loan contract, simply stick to this schedule. If you do not make enough to pay as laid out in the initial contract, you will need to talk to your lender and modify your payments. This could mean either extending the term of your loan or making graduated payments, in which you make smaller payments for a certain period of time and then make higher payments later on. In the case of graduated repayments, the term of your loan is not usually extended; it remains what it was in the initial contract.

The implications of making loan payments as per the initial contract versus modifying the contract to accommodate for difficulties in meeting the initial contract will vary. There are certainly advantages to not altering the initial contract and making payments as scheduled: you pay less in interest over the life of the loan. But then life and circumstances vary for different people. If you are in an adverse situation in which you don't get the job you planned for after college, don't hesitate to alter your repayment plan. Make a decision and act early rather than be forced to make the same decision later on, in which case you may incur financial penalties.

For example, if your first job after college does not pay you enough to be able to meet your student-loan repayment obligations, it would be prudent to talk to the lender and modify the terms to lower your monthly payment. This way, you are unlikely to incur any penalties, such as late fees.

Now if you do not talk to your lender immediately and instead default on your student loan, it creates several problems for you. It affects your credit score, and you also incur fines in the form of late fees—all of which are added to your outstanding amount. In such a case, you may eventually be forced by your lender to go for a modification but at terms that are not favorable to you. It may be difficult to refinance your loan in such circumstances, for your credit score will have been sullied. It is true that you may end up paying a lot more in interest over the life of the loan if you need to modify your initial contract, but timely modification at your own initiative may result in modification terms that are more favorable to you as opposed to a situation where modification is initiated by the lender after you have failed to make timely payments.

Once you take proactive steps based on your situation, you can focus on priorities that will help you progress in your career to increase your income and be able to pay off your loan sooner than you had initially planned. So make a repayment plan as soon as you are out of college, and focus on other priorities that will help you pay off your student loan ahead of schedule.

What Is the Estimated Time Frame Over Which I Should Repay My Student-Loan Debt?

Although it is great to be able to pay off your student loan in a short period of time, when it comes to planning, think of a conservative schedule. Plan for a longer repayment term than it might realistically take to pay off the loan. Once you are aware of the full extent of your liability, it makes sense to plan out a repayment schedule that does not require you to make too many sacrifices. A conservative estimate leaves you with a cushion in times of need. When you plan a longer repayment schedule, you are in a better position to save. If you make aggressive payments right from the beginning, it may leave you with too little or even with nothing at all to save.

When you get a job after college and your repayment period starts, make a monthly budget of your expenditures and income. The expenditures should include all expenses, such as housing, utilities, food, car loans, and all other obligations, including the student-loan payment. If you find that your income exceeds your expenditures by a comfortable margin, you can simply stick to your original repayment schedule without having to make any changes to the initial terms of the contract. If your income is much higher than your expenditures, you may even allocate an additional sum of money for your student-loan payment.

This way, you can shorten the life of your loan and be free of student-loan debt sooner than you initially planned.

Now, suppose your budgeting leaves you with a deficit, you need to consider reducing your expenses. If you still find that you don't have enough to make your student-loan payments, you will need to work with your lender and modify your repayment schedule, usually by lowering your payment and extending the term of the loan. It is typically better to extend the term of the loan and lower your monthly payments rather than go for graduated repayment plans, if you have a choice.

The problem with graduated plans is that after a certain period of time during which you can make lower payments, your payments shoot up. Now, you don't know your future. If in the future when the payments go up you don't have a higher income, you are again in a fix. However, if you choose a longer term with a lower monthly payment, you do not have to worry about an increase in your payments in the future. If over time your income increases, you can simply make higher monthly payments and shorten the life of your loan. Of course, if you have a variable-rate loan, your payments will fluctuate, and you will have to plan accordingly.

What Kind of Repayment Plan Should I Opt For?

The answer to this question will depend on your income and the quantity of debt you have incurred as a student. If your total debt is a small amount, it makes sense not to alter the original repayment schedule that was set in the contract when you took out the loan. It might even be worthwhile to prepay the loan by paying more than the monthly installment due; this will help you get out of debt in a short period of time. However, if your debt is a substantial amount, you will need to look into the different repayment options available.

Once again, if you are able to get a high-paying job immediately after college, you should stick to your original repayment schedule and try to pay off your loan as early as possible. The sooner you pay off your student loan, the better off you are, as you will be able to use the amount of money allocated to your monthly student-loan payment for other purposes once it is paid off. Now, if your debt is a substantial amount and your income is not sufficient to make payments as per the original repayment schedule, you will need to explore different possibilities.

You only need to alter your repayment plan if you want to lower your monthly payments and lengthen the repayment term. There is no need to alter the repayment plan if you want to shorten the life of the loan. Simply make additional payment along with the monthly installment.

Just make sure that your loan contract does not include a prepayment penalty. When students take out loans, they are thinking about paying their college tuition, attending classes, or simply enjoying the college life and not about the implications that their student-loan debt might have in the future. Moreover, in most cases, they are simply too young to understand the ramifications of the contract they are entering into. They do not explore the details and instead overlook the fine print of the contract until they receive their first bill, or even later.

As mentioned earlier, when you make plans for your repayment schedule, consider the total debt (i.e., the outstanding principal balance and the total amount in interest you expect to pay over the term of the loan). When it comes to income, consider your net income—the income you take home after all deductions. It may be unwise to consider your gross income in your calculations, for you will never take home your deductions.

Here are a few typical scenarios to consider and the option to choose in each scenario:

➢ If your total debt is less than your net annual income, try not to make any changes to your original repayment schedule. Instead, pay off your loan as soon as possible. For example, if your net annual income is $40,000 and your total student loan debt is $20,000, stick to the original repayment schedule.

> If your total debt is roughly equal to your net annual income, it still makes sense to stick to the original schedule. If you need to lower your payment in such cases, owing to other obligations, go for a graduated repayment plan. This way, you are not extending the term of your loan and can still take care of your short-term obligations. You should not have problems when your payment goes up in the future, for the total debt is not a substantial amount, and your paycheck is likely to increase as you gain experience.

> If your total debt is more than one and a half to two times your net annual income, consider modifying your loan to lower your payments. For example, if your annual income is $40,000, your total student-loan debt is $60,000, and your repayment term is fifteen years, it may make sense to opt for a slightly longer term so you can save more money in the early stages of your career. Now if your net annual income is $40,000 and your student loan debt is $80,000 and the repayment term is fifteen years, it would be wise to extend the term of your loan to twenty years or more. Of course, in either case, you will have some negotiation to do with your lender to work out a deal that is best for you.

> If your total debt is more than three times your net annual income, you are in a strong need of debt counseling right at the outset. Not only will you

need to modify your loan payments, but also you should request the maximum extension possible as far as your repayment term goes.

➢ Now, a special-case scenario arises if you have a cosigner for your student loan and you want to release the cosigner. In such cases, try to stick to the original repayment schedule for at least the first two years. This repayment schedule was set when you initially signed the note. Many student loans have cosigners, and the release of the cosigner is contingent upon your making on-time payments based on the original repayment schedule for at least two years. Many lenders are very stubborn about this indenture clause, and should you want to be relieved of the cosigner, this is your best bet. Once you have released the cosigner from your debt, you can work with your lender to change the repayment plan should the need arise.

These are just a few examples to get you started. Depending on your situation, you may need to look at other options. Remember, in all the cases above, aim for a conservative repayment plan that gives you the ability to save starting with your very first paycheck. If you save even a little, it adds up over time, and in the future, these savings may help you pay off your student loan much sooner than you initially anticipated when you finished college.

Moreover, in all the above cases, you can pay a higher amount than the monthly amount owed if your income increases as you move up in your career. You also get to deduct a portion of the interest paid off your taxes so your annual tax bill will be lower because of your student loan repayment than it would be without it. The key to picking the right repayment term is to balance the student-loan payments with other obligations and necessities in life.

What Percentage of My Income Should I Devote to Repaying My Student Loan?

You can be aggressive with your payments if your income is much higher than anticipated. Otherwise, prepare a conservative repayment schedule by making sure that under no circumstances your monthly student-loan payment exceeds 15 to 20 percent of your take-home income. Twenty percent is an extreme case, and it would make sense to keep your loan payment no higher than 10 percent of your take-home pay. If you should ever find yourself making a monthly student-loan payment that is more than 20 percent of your net monthly income, you are in serious need of debt restructuring and debt counseling.

Mind you, the percentages I am referring to are percentages of your net income, not your gross income. If you calculate these percentages of your gross income before taxes and deductions, you will have very little left from your take-home pay after making the loan payments. Allocating a small percentage of your take-home pay to your student loan payment leaves you with money for savings, among other things. Get into the habit of saving, however little it may be, for it all adds up, and before you know it, you will find that you have a decent bank balance that will come in handy for a rainy day.

Let us consider the different scenarios one by one:

➢ If your monthly student-loan payment is less than 10 percent of your monthly net income, you are in a comfortable situation. Even if you can afford to, do not make too many additional payments toward paying off your student loan. Make small additional payments, and hold off on making large additional payments every month for some time. Save the additional amount, or invest it wisely. You can start making substantial additional payments every month when your income increases.

➢ If your monthly student-loan payment lies within 15 to 20 percent of your monthly net income, you are in a tight situation. Consider this a short-term situation, and look for other options. One option is to look to improve your income situation, which could mean looking for another job that pays more. Another option is to work with your lender and modify the payment terms, resulting in a lower monthly payment that falls at or below 10 percent of your monthly net income.

➤ If your monthly student-loan payment is more than 20 percent of your monthly net income, you definitely need to modify your loan. It also means that the job you are in does not befit your qualifications, and you should start looking for a job that is in line with your skills. The first step in this case is to work with the lender and get some short-term relief in the form of lower monthly payments; the second but more important step is to aggressively look for another job that pays better and is more in line with what you went to school for.

Always remember that while it is great to pay off your student loan as early as possible, it should not come at the price of making sacrifices and forgoing many good things that life has to offer. There should be a balance between debt repayments and finding happiness. You should be as aggressive about saving as you are about repaying your student loan and discover the proper balance between the two.

What Kind of jobs Should I Be Targeting in Both the Short and Medium Terms to Help Me Pay Off My Loan?

The job that you end up with after college will decide the fate of your student-loan repayment. A well-paying job will help you pay off your student loans with a high degree of comfort, whereas a not-so-cushy job may leave you struggling as you try to pay off your loan. The key to future comfort and happiness is finding the right job, and that means targeting the appropriate jobs when you are ready to hit the job market.

Your job-search strategy should have both a short-term and a long-term perspective. Your very first job out of college may not pay well, but it gives you the footing you need for a successful career. When you start looking for jobs, the repayment of your student loan should be at the back of your mind, for you do not want to default on this obligation right at the outset and face the bitter consequences. With any kind of default, it takes years to get your life back to normal, and you do not want to be in that situation.

Before you start looking for jobs, determine the extent of your student-loan liability by calculating your total outstanding debt, including the interest owed over the life of the loan term, and the immediate short-term monthly installment payments you will incur as soon as the repayment term begins. Now you should think of the 10 percent criterion mentioned earlier—that is, you want to allocate no more than 10 percent of your net monthly income to your monthly student-loan repayment. This calculation will give you an idea of your target salary range.

When looking for jobs, target a high salary range and then bring your expectations down, depending on the results of your search as you go. Look for jobs in companies that are seeking someone with your educational qualifications, and then look at the pay scale they are offering for those jobs. This will give you a fairly good idea of where you stand.

Try not to divert your job search toward jobs that are seeking candidates with qualifications different from your educational credentials. You chose your coursework based on certain expectations about what you wanted to do in the future. Unless the alternative options are rosy, it would be sensible to stay on your chosen path. Stay on track except if you encounter a dead end at every juncture of a job search that is in line with your qualifications. You will have the best chance of convincing a hiring manager of your eligibility for a job when it requires someone with your qualifications.

In the short term, look for jobs that meet your expected pay scales. If you are unable to get any offers that are up to your expectations, you may need to modify your job-search criteria. If at the end of your trials you land a job that matches or exceeds your expectations, you are well on course to meeting your student-loan repayment obligations without much hassle. If after all your efforts you end up with a job that is not up to your salary expectations, you will need to modify your student-loan repayment plan or be prepared to make sacrifices in the short term in order to stick to your repayment schedule.

Now, in some situations, despite your best efforts, you may not be able to get a job after graduation. In such a case, work immediately with your lender, and explore options that will help you get some relief. Do not let any opportunity for debt relief slip simply because you did not act on time.

The long-term dimension of your job-search strategy is to first make sure that the job you end up in after graduation is in line with fulfilling your career aspirations, one of the major aspirations being an increase in pay as time progresses. Now, there may be individuals for whom an increase in pay over time is not one of their primary objectives. You could well be one of them. However, if you have a student-loan debt and your current job does not pay you enough to comfortably make your student-loan payments, then you will have no choice but to work toward increasing your pay. You can always cater to your major aspirations once you have paid off your debt.

Suppose your first job after college is not up to your expectations but you end up taking it all the same, owing to financial obligations and to sustain yourself. You will need to plan your long-term strategy well. You will also need to work hard, prove yourself, and build up skills that will help you move into the job that you aspire to in the future.

This is easier said than done and may require many sacrifices. For example, you may need to work longer hours to prove yourself and gain the skills that are essential for your progress. The end result could be a hike in pay in your current job or finding a job that matches your expectations. Either way, you will do better to pay off your student loan without encountering much discomfort or distress.

Just keep in mind that no matter what kind of job you end up with after college, it should help you pay off your student loan as planned. In case of adversities, think of your distress as short term in nature. In the short term, make the minimum payments owed even if it requires some sacrifices. Look for something better in the long term by developing skills and building up experience that will help you get there. Once you attain your long-term goal, your comfort level will increase, and the repayment of student loan will not be a big issue.

In Case of Adversities, What Backup Plan Should I Have to Make My Student-Loan Payments?

Time and again in this chapter, I have emphasized the importance of saving, starting with your first paycheck. Even if you save only a small fraction of your paycheck, over time it adds up and comes in handy in times of adversity.

We can never really plan completely for setbacks. The day we are able to do that, we will not face adversities in the first place. However, we can make contingency plans that may help us face setbacks without losing too much.

Adversity could include anything, from a temporary loss of job and income to something long term, such as a health issue. In order to take care of long-term impairment of income owing to health-related issues, insurance policies are available that can help tide you over during the crisis. When you get a job, look at the different insurance and protection plans the company offers in addition to health, dental, and vision insurance. When you explore these options, you may come across plans that help you prepare for such situations.

Carefully evaluate all plans and options available, and pick one with premium payments that do not hurt you much financially. It is always a good idea to go with plans that are offered or sponsored by the company you work for and ones that are payroll deducted. Looking for plans not sponsored by your employer can be an expensive proposition, one that cuts too much into your paycheck.

We tend to ignore these insurance options when we start a new job and during the early stages of adult life. However, good planning for contingencies right from the beginning always comes in handy, so do explore these options when you get your first job or, for that matter, at any stage of your life.

Short-term adversities are typically temporary loss of income owing to job layoff or termination of employment. In such cases, in addition to looking for full-time employment or any means of gainful income generation, you will have to make sure to keep your credit history intact or avoid doing maximum damage to it. At these times, you need to talk to your lender and modify your payment terms.

One alternative is an interest-only payment option, which would bring down your monthly payments substantially. This payment option is a temporary solution and is possible if you have savings. If you have no savings and are in the unfortunate situation of being out of a job, making student-loan payments is more or less an impossible proposition. The best course of action in such cases is opting for deferment or forbearance, which allows you to postpone making payments for a short period of time.

Of course, this action is subject to your lender's approval and will have long-term ramifications. It may affect your credit, and your debt also starts to mount, for the interest accrued over this period and any potential fines are all added to your outstanding debt. Eventually, when you are ready again for repayment, you are left with a far-higher liability than when you ceased making payments. So go for this deferment or forbearance option only as a last resort when you have exhausted all other avenues.

Given the adversities that we may have to face in life, be prepared for any eventuality. Always be optimistic—hope for the best, but be prepared for the worst. Think of any setback or shock as a temporary phenomenon, and believe that you will get back on track once you have endured it. When you plan for adversities, it is much easier to absorb the shock, and in the case of student-loan repayments, you can ride out the crisis without too much damage.

How Do I Balance My Student-Loan Repayment with the Repayment of Other Debts That I Might Incur in the Course of My Life?

Throughout life, we will have to make many investments as the need arises. Having student loan debt should not get in the way of these investments. The key to it all is balancing our budget. For example, it would be unwise to postpone buying a home when a good investment opportunity presents itself just because we have student-loan debt.

Likewise, should we postpone all spending because we have a student loan debt? The answer is a big no. We need to make investments and spend money whenever a good opportunity arises. After all, we incurred a student loan hoping it would help us better our lives, and the key to betterment is finding happiness.

Postponing certain activities in life because of other obligations may not always be a wise idea. The home that you forgo today because of your student-loan repayment obligation may be a lot more expensive when you are eventually ready for it. The alternative at the time would be to settle for a home that is not your dream home but just a residence—a roof over your head. Imagine realizing in the future that you could have bought your dream home at the very first opportunity at a low price, balanced your budget, and still paid off your student loan! How would you feel then? Definitely not pleased.

So the best thing you can do is to balance your budget, allocate a certain fraction of your income toward repaying your student loan, and still make wise investments when the opportunities present themselves. As I mentioned earlier in this chapter, allocating no more than 10 percent of your net income to your student-loan repayment will leave you enough to save, and these savings will help you make investments when opportunities arise.

Of course, there may be times when you are left with no option but to allocate more than 10 percent of your income to meeting your student-loan repayment obligations. These times should be temporary in nature; otherwise, you will need to talk to your lender and work out a satisfactory solution. Make investments that you can afford and that are well within your budget. Do not go for frivolous stuff if you cannot afford it yet.

When you make wise investments, you will incur additional debt besides your student loan. For example, it is highly unlikely that you will buy a home without a mortgage. If you can afford one without a mortgage, it would be wiser to pay off your student loan with a fraction of that money and invest the remainder in your dream home. If after budgeting and saving you have money left over, make additional payments toward the loan that incurs the highest interest. Get rid of your costly debt first, and then focus on the lower-cost debts.

At various stages in your life, and as long as you have student loan or any debt remaining, you will need to make a budget and stick to its schedule. This will help you lead a better quality of life. As with everything else, planning and budgeting are very important!

Before concluding this chapter, let's consider the best- and worst-case scenarios for variable-rate student loans—and, for that matter, for all student loans. In the best-case scenario, the variable-rate student loans carry a low interest rate, which effectively means low monthly payments. This gives you the opportunity to pay off the loan quickly by making more than the minimum payment owed every month.

However, the rates are low when the overall interest rates in the financial markets are low because of a depressed economy. The challenge here is to stay employed, take full advantage of the low interest rates, and get rid of the student-loan debt earlier than planned. In the worst-case scenario, the interest rates and thus the monthly loan payments for variable-rate loans are high.

However, there is a silver lining in such a situation. Interest rates tend to be high when the economy is doing well, and there are plenty of high-paying jobs available. So even though the monthly payments are high, it would not hurt much to make the payments when your paycheck is higher. The key in all cases is staying employed and wisely using the opportunities that present themselves.

Remember, your student loan is more of an asset than a liability. You incurred the student loan to equip yourself with an education that you expected would provide you with a good job. So make full use of this tool, and if you encounter challenging situations, face the challenges head-on, for only then will you win the battles of life. Whatever the case, understand the full extent of your liability, including your interest payments, and then devise a repayment plan that suits *you*, as opposed to the one set out in the contract you signed when you took out the student loan.

If you have a student loan, over the long term, you are better off with it than you would have been without it. Realize this and make full use of the tools you gained via your education that was made possible by your student loan.

CONCLUSION

Finally, I would like to reiterate the importance of finding the means to provide the basic necessities to sustain yourself: a roof over your head, food on the table, and a source of income to support all your other minimum needs. It is only when you possess these basic items that you can think of building on your dreams.

Whether we like it or not, it is a fact that we live in a highly competitive world in which we always need to plan and be competitive in order to survive, sustain ourselves, and move ahead. Absent our basic requirements, relaxation is a distant dream. In order to meet those basic requirements, we need to have skills that we can use to obtain some form of income. A decent education or knowledge of some kind of trade that has demand in the market will give us the opportunity to look for a job that can help us sustain ourselves.

While some people have achieved great success without any kind of formal education, this isn't possible for most people. In order to be eligible for jobs, most people need training or education that will enable them to find work and make a living. In order to meet your minimum requirements and then convert your dreams into reality, you need a solid foundation.

Success in any venture depends on the foundation and groundwork that goes into it. A solid foundation gives you the platform on which you can build your career; the hard work that you put in will help you move toward your goals. Your hard work is the ladder that will allow you to climb up. While the ladder itself has to be strong, the ground on which you place the ladder has to be firm—only then will the ladder find a solid footing.

The solid ground in your endeavor is your planning and focus. The better you plan and the more focused you are, the firmer your footing. With a firm footing, your hard work will help you achieve your goals. Without good planning, resolve, and drive before you even start a venture, all your hard work might go to waste. That's why you need to plan well before starting your endeavors, for absent planning and focus, all your best efforts may not yield the desired results.

Never start any venture without knowing what you are getting into. Never start working on something without knowing the result you desire. Whatever you want to do, think before you begin—do not do it simply for the sake of doing it or just because somebody suggested it without giving the slightest heed to your own interests. Your planning might not be perfect, but it will still help you get on the right track. You may have doubts in your mind; when you do, seek help.

A bad plan can be corrected and perfected as you work toward your goals and carve out your path. However, not having any plan will simply leave you without a goal, and not having a goal will set you adrift. Whatever you want to do in life, plan and take baby steps to achieve your dreams. Don't expect too much in too short a time. You can aim for big things, but you should temper your wishes with tinges of reality.

Keep your plans simple to begin with, and start by doing things one step at a time. As you progress along your path, the way will become clearer—that's when you can plan big. Don't think that once you make a plan, you are done with planning. You can have a grand plan, but in order for that grand plan to become a reality, you need to have a miniplan for every step of the way. It is only when you plan before each step that you can deal with contingencies.

Never lose focus, for the consequences that follow are not pleasant. Many people begin their endeavors with a good plan. However, when they face obstacles, they tend to lose focus and drift from their goals. Focus is critical to achievement. In many sports—like football, soccer, or basketball—it is important to keep your eyes on the ball. All the hard work and skills of the players concerned would amount to nothing if they failed to keep their eyes on the ball. Having focus as you set out to achieve your goals is like keeping your eyes on the ball. No matter what you set out to do, keep your goal in mind. Having that vision of your goal will help you reach it. Even if you struggle sometimes, your path to your goal will get clearer.

Do not be intimidated by the competition you may encounter on the way. Simply think about what you need to do to achieve your goal. In the process, you can overcome the competition. For example, in order to get admitted into a top school, you need to focus on how high you must score on a standardized test like the SAT, GRE, or GMAT rather than think about how many people you have to beat in order to do so. If you get a very high score, your competition will automatically fall by the wayside. Focusing on your goals rather than worrying about the noise along the way will help you do what you need to in order to achieve your goals.

Always believe in yourself, and keep moving ahead. Never doubt your abilities, and do not ever think that you will not succeed. If you think that you cannot succeed, simply do not venture out. I often hear people use phrases like "Given my luck, I do not expect anything positive to come out of this venture." Never think that way. Even if you have encountered bad luck earlier, believe that your luck will start changing for the better. Positive thinking will always make things easier for you. So plan ahead, believe in yourself, have faith in your abilities, work hard, and maintain focus and drive, and you will succeed in your venture.

APPENDIX I

AN EXAMPLE OF AN EXPERIENCED PROFESSIONAL'S RÉSUMÉ

SOMEBODY SOMEWHERE
100 Somewhere Ln • Any City, Any State 11111 • (111) 222-331 • someone@somemail.com

---

— MANAGEMENT CONSULTANT —

Strategic planner and consultant in diverse product and service enterprises seeking a position to excel in and create incremental value for the organization

- Demonstrate expertise in planning with sophistication in analysis, leading to enhanced revenues and profitability, asset growth, loss mitigation, risk management, and customer satisfaction.

- Forecasting and analyses of asset price movements and communicating with different parties to mitigate risk

- Secure and maximize key business relationships and strategic partnerships

- Coordinate internal and external entities toward achievement of corporate mission

- Advance time-sensitive multitiered agendas in challenging environments

- Identify and seize opportunities to expand role of assignment

- Ability to multitask and handle multiple ad hoc requests

KEY COMPETENCIES

• Product Strategy • Business and Financial Modeling • Operational Excellence • ROI
Revenue Generation and Savings • Budget Control • Analysis • Data Management • Forecasting • Asset Protection
Risk Management • Loss Mitigation • Capital Funding and Restructuring • Market Expansions • Client Acquisition and Retention

Goal Setting • Needs Assessments • Resource Allocations
• Portfolio Dynamics • Benchmarking
Communications • Presentations • Streamlining
• Negotiations • Change Management •
Consensus Building • Problem Solving

— PROFESSIONAL EXPERIENCE —

BIG COMPANY INC.,
Any City, Any State Jan. 2010–Present
Multinational diversified consumer products company

Management Consultant

Met challenges in an ever-changing business scenario with zeal and positive energy and completed all assigned tasks with thorough due diligence within the set time frames and with maximum impact

- Responsible for generating, compiling, and ensuring accuracy of multiple actionable reports on a daily, weekly, and monthly basis for executive management to enable decision making
- Coordinated with several cross-functional teams and management to both troubleshoot and improve efficiency of various processes

- Made significant impact in a short span of time as a troubleshooter and go-getter who can be relied upon to deliver results timely and efficiently while maintaining high standards and minimizing risk exposure

- Successfully initiated changes to streamline departmental operations while motivating team members to achieve high degrees of excellence

- Conceived and implemented ideas that resulted in elevated levels of coordination across various teams, thus improving performance standards and achieving company objectives of superior performance levels and risk minimization

SOMEBODY SOMEWHERE
someone@somemail.com • Page 2

- Created techniques for loss mitigation and minimizing risk exposure, resulting in savings of 2 percent

- Innovated model for forecasting and budgeting of corporate advances, resulting in reduction of cost of capital by 1 percent

- Modified and automated processes at corporate headquarters, resulting in time savings as well as revenue equivalent of monthly wages of ten full-time employees

- Analyzed global supplier performance system data to facilitate trend analysis, determining performance of suppliers

- Prepared electronic commodity pricing data for improved global commodity negotiation processes

MIDSIZED COMPANY INC.,
Midcity, Midstate 2005 –2009
Diversified consumer products company

Junior Management Consultant, Operations and Administration

Met challenges to compete with global competition through achievement of corporate-wide consensus for business development initiatives, as well as operations, finance, and sales improvement. Optimized operations through oversight of facilities, office, inventory, supply chain, purchasing, shipping, distribution, and customer support.

- Introduced concept for establishment of company-owned retail outlets while expanding sales to additional retailers and maintaining business with existent wholesaler base, resulting in sales boost of 50 percent

- Negotiated with suppliers of raw material to extend period of credit while encouraging end-customers to purchase product on cash with discount, resulting in improved inventory turnover and 8 percent reduction in operating costs

- Facilitated opening of retail outlets, maximized production capacity, and saved interest costs by 3 percent through capital restructuring
- Analyzed process flow to assess cost involved in returned products

— EDUCATION —

MBA, Marketing, University of Midstate, Midcity, Midstate

BE, Mechanical Engineering, Small State University, Small City, Small State

— CERTIFICATION —

Project Management Certification, Visual Studio

—TECHNICAL SKILLS —

Microsoft Office Visual Studio Project Management SQL Database Management

APPENDIX II

EXAMPLE OF A RECENT COLLEGE GRADUATE'S RÉSUMÉ

SOMEBODY SOMEWHERE
100 Somewhere Ln, Apartment 9999
Any City, Any State 11111
111-222-3333
someone@somemail.com

OBJECTIVE

Hardworking, committed young professional seeking a position with a reputable firm with opportunities for growth and development

EDUCATION

UNIVERSITY OF MID STATE – Midstate College of
Business
Bachelor of Science, Midcity, Midstate   May 2013

Concentration: Marketing GPA 3.72
Relevant Coursework

- Global Marketing
- Relationship Marketing
- Business Marketing I
- Executive Sales Management
- Advertising Management
- Marketing Research
- Business Marketing II
- Brand Strategy

EXPERIENCE

Market Research Analyst   June 2013–Present
Small Company, Inc., Small City, Small State

- Collection, compilation, and analysis of consumer data to assess supplier performance in different industries
- Preparation of reports for suppliers' use in self-analysis, planning, training, and improvement
- Study, design, implementation, and preparation of reports based on consumer behavior in different industries
- Presentation of market study and consumer behavior to clients for improving their marketing strategy
- Designing of marketing models based on client requirements and market assessment

Marketing Intern   Summer 2012
Internship, Inc., Midcity, Midstate

- Analyzed global supplier performance system data to facilitate trend analysis determining performance of the supplier
- Prepared commodity pricing data to better facilitate global commodity negotiation processes
- Analyzed process flow to assess cost involved in returned products

Shift Supervisor   Jul 2008–Jul 2009
Small Town Restaurant, Small City, Small State

- Responsible for providing quality service and customer satisfaction
- Responsible for planning and organizing cleaning agendas to maintain levels of cleanliness appropriate for health inspections
- Gained reputation for being trustworthy, a team player, and leadership ability

COMPUTER AND OTHER SKILLS

Microsoft Word, Excel, Access, PowerPoint, and Money Guide Pro

HONORS AND ACTIVITIES

Social service and charitable activities volunteer,
Small City Volunteers Association   2012–Present
Relief Society Member, ABC Charity Trust   2012–Present
Dean's List, University of Midstate   2009–2011

ABOUT THE AUTHOR

Shiva Lakota is based in Charlotte, North Carolina. He is a well-qualified individual and has a flourishing career. After his own share of failures at various junctures in his earlier life, over time, he learned that in order to succeed, he needed to have the will to do so and the willingness to work for those achievements.

When he changed his outlook on life, success followed. Moreover, his positive outlook ensures that he is always happy. *Building Your Career: Laying the Foundation to Fulfill Your Dreams* was written to share this philosophy and to spread the author's simple, effective method of achieving success, personal fulfillment, and the ultimate diamond ring—true happiness.

CPSIA information can be obtained
at www.ICGtesting.com
Printed in the USA
LVOW04s2054120816
500060LV00016B/186/P